CELTIC SAINTS

THE NEW CELTIC LIBRARY

Series Editor
Stuart Booth

•

The Celtic Tradition
David James

Celtic Saints
Dr. Bob Curran

The Celtic Cross
Nigel Pennick

Celtic Pilgrimages
Elaine Gill & Rev. David Everett

The Celtic Druids
Yowann Byghan

THE NEW CELTIC LIBRARY

•

CELTIC SAINTS

Bob Curran

ST DAVID'S PRESS

Published in Wales in 2007 by St David's Press
an imprint of

Ashley Drake Publishing Ltd
PO Box 725
Cardiff
CF14 2YX
www.ashleydrake.com

A CIP catalogue for this book is available from the British Library

ISBN: 978 1 902719 15 3

Typeset by Mudra Typesetters

Printed in Malta by Gutenberg Press Limited

CONTENTS

INTRODUCTION

Although it would appear that the underlying perspective of Western Christian religion has remained fairly constant across the centuries – humanity's relationship with an all-powerful, all-embracing God – it remains equally true that there have been a number of standpoints regarding that relationship. As Christianity changed from the belief of a persecuted minority into a fully-fledged and organized religion, competing perspectives and impulses vied for the control of the Christian outlook. Two fundamental questions exercised the early Christian mind.

Firstly, how could the individual most profitably enjoy the relationship with his or her God? Was this to be best achieved through communal and public ritual or through private reflection and self-examination? Secondly, how did the fledgling Church react to the pagan world that surrounded it?

It has to be remembered that those who had converted to Christianity had initially been pagans themselves, and that at least some pagan values and interpretations had been passed down through succeeding years. It must also be remembered that because of the temperament and character of the peoples involved, the Christian perspective often varied from location to location. It is not surprising, then, that several strands of Christianity – several responses to God – began to emerge across the ancient world. One of these was the Celtic Church.

There were a number of elements which marked the distinctiveness of Celtic Christianity. The first of these was emergence of a personalized response that concentrated upon an individual rather than communal worship. This is not to say that there was not a social element as well; but the underlying ethos lay in a direct relationship with God, rather than one that was heavily mediated by an organized external Church. This, of course, led to the lack of a strong and centralized institution. By viewing personal sanctity as more important that institutional and doctrinal uniformity, the Celtic Church was less authoritarian, more decentralized and ultimately more fragmented than its Roman counterpart. Again, such a viewpoint led to inconsistencies and eccentricities within the Church, yet with its emphasis on spirituality it has come to be regarded as perhaps a more 'pure' form of religion than the orthodox dogmas that succeeded it.

As to the second element, one of the central tenets of Celtic Christianity was the expression of individual's relationship with God as best achieved through a closeness with the natural world. Much of the Celtic experience was rooted in the landscape – the Celts had been initially hunters and latterly farmers – and so it was only to be expected that Celtic worship should reflect this aspect. This fitted in well with the notion of withdrawal from urban centres, into isolated, rural settings in order to reflect and meditate. It is also to be found in the importance of animals and plants in the lives and legends of the Celtic saints. Crops, the elements, seasons, regeneration and procreation, land, ocean, sky and stars were all manifestations of God and were part of His plan. The way in which the soil was tended, animals were cared for, natural resources were protected all served as examples of Humanity's relationship with the Creator of All Things. In the western world of today, our own commodity-orientated society, together with our mismanagement of the world around us would have appalled and disturbed all of the early saints who would have considered our modern society to be inherently blasphemous.

A third element which marked the Celtic Church was

the allegedly covert continuance of an inherently pagan outlook. In many parts of the Celtic world, Christianity sought to oust much older and strongly established beliefs. These beliefs included the worship of spirits and forces at such places as wells, stone and other such sites dotted across the landscape and were largely controlled and regulated by recognized pagan priests known as Druids. Although relatively haphazard, the Druid religion still had sufficient inherent structure to allow the Christian religion to merge with it and develop around it. Both religions adapted, feeding into one another. There was a still a strong sense of the miraculous within the Celtic Christian tradition and ancient pagan wells and enclosures now became associated with Christian saints and worship at such sites continued. Only now it was not a pagan deity that was worshipped there, it was the person of some holy man or woman. Pagan feast days also assumed religious connotations and most of the great religious feasts in, say, the Irish calendar correspond with more ancient pagan festivals. A tradition of clairvoyance for religious purposes – for example to foretell the coming of Christ – was encouraged, as was the art of 'wonderworking' (achieving supernatural ends through the power of Christ). This of course, led the Roman Church to describe the Celtic religious tradition as 'pagans by another name'.

This leads to the fourth characteristic of the Celtic Church – a highly mystical approach to the religious. Rather than concentrating exclusively on dogma, ritual and orthodoxy, Celtic clerics tended to look towards the etheric and supernatural. They saw visions, heard voices, made predictions, and glimpsed the nearness of a mystical Otherworld. These were dismissed and derided by the Roman church as occult and magical practices. Yet, such allegations may have been motivated by the jealousy of formal ecclesiastical hierarchies in order to suppress any competition to their doctrines. In order to promote their own world view, they deliberately confused the mystical calling, which many of these saints experienced, with the workings of the shamans and druids of pagan times.

And so, two strands of Christian doctrine began to grow in the Celtic West: the Celtic strand, with its emphasis on individual sanctity; and mystical tradition and the Roman one, laying stress on unity, dogma and centralized structures. The Roman tradition was centred upon Rome, whilst the Celtic had its base on the island of Iona, off Western Scotland. The Celtic tradition embraced – amongst others – the Irish, Scottish, Welsh, Cornish, North English and Breton spheres of influence. So, although fragmented in nature, it had an impact far into Europe. Consequently, the two traditions competed with each other for converts to Christianity.

The matter was reputedly settled at the Synod of Whitby in AD 664, with the Roman tradition assuming dominance. This was not surprising, as its structure and organization was modeled on and lent itself to the political and military hierarchies of the medieval world. The closeness of Church and State would become a significant feature of the developing culture of the Middle Ages.

Contrastingly, the Celtic Church was too diffuse, less authoritarian and without a centralized doctrine, which could be readily enforced. It therefore held little interest for the political system of the day. Even though Rome was now in the ascendancy, elements of the Celtic tradition persisted down across the years, ingraining themselves deeply in the Western religious psyche.

Today, in a world which is once more beginning to stress individuality and the 'quest for self' the Celtic standpoint is perhaps of more interest although the rigor of its asceticism might not be so appealing. The expression of the religious relationship may find echoes in the 'green movement' of today though it is doubtful as to whether modern adherents would wish to give up all comforts to endure the privations of the hermit life. It is tempting to look back on the 'Age of Saints' as some lost golden era when all was blissful and tranquil, yet their world was in some ways as harsh and fraught as our own. For the hermits and cenobites, each day was in all probability an ordeal which few of us could survive for long and their mysticism was as much a retreat from the tribulations of everyday life as it was from the distractions of civilization.

In preparing a book on the saints, the writer is faced with a number of difficulties. Foremost is the fact that we have to depend on the *Lives of ... ...*. Many of these accounts were written long after the death of a particular saint, and – for the most part – are both scant on detail and inaccurate. Next is the fact that we have to disentangle myth from fact, since most of the material which we have on these holy people is little more than legend and anecdote. It is not always an easy task to detail important Celtic saints in a manner that demonstrates how their Church developed but was ultimately subsumed by the orthodoxy of Rome.

Nevertheless, that is what I have tried to do and – as far as possible – tried to show the historical figure and his or her importance to the Church of the time. Here is a mixture of historical fact, legend, folktale and personal anecdote, which I hope will coalesce into a picture of a fascinating and spiritual era.

If you have obtained an intriguing glimpse of a unique and complex Church, and if you have experienced something of the awe and wonder of those early Celtic Christians, then I have succeeded.

Dr Robert Curran
Co. Derry, 2003

Chapter 1

THE DESERT FATHERS

There seems little doubt that early Celtic Christian saints took, as their inspiration the lives of the Desert Fathers, who tried to develop a relationship with God, deep in the inhospitable wastes of the Egyptian deserts. The mortification of the flesh through the harshness of the existence coupled with the inherent mysticism which came from the intense isolation, found an echo in the Celtic spirit and many of the founders of the Celtic Church and the early monasticists (and indeed others besides) sought to emulate their way of life.

The phrase 'Desert Fathers' refers to an influential group of fourth-century hermits and cenobites who had largely withdrawn from the everyday world to retreat into the deserts to commune better with God. Their lives were centered on intense prayer and contemplation away from the distractions of civilization. By their example and teachings they laid the foundations of Western monasticism and established a tradition of personal asceticism that so appealed to the Celtic Christian ideal.

The earliest of these ascetics is recorded as Paul of Thebes (who allegedly lived AD 230–342 and died aged 112) although the father of cenobitism or early monasticism is given as Pachomius of Thebiad in Upper Egypt who died around the year 325. Although he certainly became a hermit around the year 317, he also founded several colonies of like-minded recluses and wrote a Rule that balanced community with the solitary life. The monks lived individual lives in scattered cells and caves but occasionally came together for prayer and to work for the common good of the community. His first colony was established in Tabenna near the Nile in AD 323 and when Pachomius died, he was thought to have been the spiritual leader for nearly 3,000 hermit monks.

The most famous of all the Desert Fathers is, however, St. Anthony of Egypt, supposedly born in the year 251 in Koma, Middle Egypt and dying on Mount Colzen in 356, at the age of 105. He is described as the Patriarch of All Monks and was a disciple of Paul of Thebes. Orphaned at 20, he withdrew into the mountains becoming a solitary at the age of 35. His first hermitage was on Mount Pispir, where he suffered visions and torments from the Devil, mainly concerning carnal lusts, which many artists have tried to capture on canvas. Pispir and Arsinoe were later to become hermit colonies dedicated to the saint. These colonies supported themselves by simple work – the making of baskets and brushes – and thus the foundations of monasticism were laid. Anthony only left his hermitage once; to travel to Alexandria to fight the heresy of Arianism but for the majority of his later life lived in an isolated mountain community.

Although it is thought that the primary impulse to isolation amongst the Desert Fathers had been to avoid Christian persecution by pagans, the Edict of Milan issued in the year 313 by the Emperor Constantine changed that. This decreed that Christianity was now to be tolerated, granted legal status and was to be protected. It marked a subtle shift in the view of the Desert Fathers. No longer was the enemy an official persecutor; rather it was an intangible evil, which could only be defeated through earnest prayer and contemplation. Gradually, these communities were sought out by a growing number of Christians for their sagacity and their sacred sayings. It was thought that in the fastness of the mountains or the deserts, they could commune directly with God and so receive his wisdom.

It was probably St. John Cassian (about AD 360–433), a Romanian monk, who brought the perspectives of the Desert Fathers to the Western Celtic world. Together with a friend, Germanus, he and lived and worked in Bethlehem but was intrigued by tales of the Desert Fathers and had left for Egypt to study with them. He had become influenced by the teachings of Evagrius Ponticus, a fairly radical hermit and in the year 400, he was in Constantinople where he was a disciple and zealous defender of St. John Chrysostom, a former hermit who had become archbishop there. He was also ordained here as a deacon. When Chryssosium was deposed as archbishop, Cassian traveled to Marseilles in Gaul (France) bringing with him the teachings and outlook of the hermit monks. It was in Gaul that he established two religious houses – one for men and one for women. St. Patrick is said to have studied within one of these foundations at Lerins. These establishments were to form the basis for the spread of a mystical monastic tradition amongst the Celts.

Using the framework that Cassian had established, another East European monk, Martin of Tours (who lived 316–397), began to spread the monastic ideal by founding communities of followers away from urban centers and in remoter areas. This ideal was taken up by the Celtic saints of the fifth and sixth centuries who founded their establishments in wild and inhospitable regions just ass the Desert Fathers had done over a hundred years before. Because of the strong Celtic affinity with the natural world, such places suited their religious temperament and allowed for the prayer and contemplation that had been a feature of the hermit life.

Of course, there were no deserts in the Western world but by choosing high mountains, sea-bound islands and inaccessible promontories, the early monks managed to achieve something akin to the isolation and hardship that the early cenobites had experienced. Remote monastic communities such as Skellig Michael – a bare and towering finger of rock rising out of the ocean off the Irish coast – bear testimony to the privations and resilience of these early Christians. Solitaries frequently lived in caves and cells whilst early monasteries took the form of *clochans* (beehive huts) clustered round a single oratory. Remnants of these still remain on remote islands and the isolated places of retreat such as St. Ninian's Cave in Scotland, St. Kevin's Cave in Wicklow or St. Sennan's community on Scattery Island off the coast of County Clare in Ireland. In such places monks and hermits could mystically commune with the forces, which they felt shaped their world – an underlying and important perspective that directed the Celtic Church.

The founding impulse of Celtic Christianity, then, lay in a tradition which stretched all the way back to the Desert Fathers of Egypt. It beheld a vision of God in the natural world and suggested that the most effective way to worship Him was through prayer and meditation. It placed an emphasis upon personal reflection and privation; it stressed withdrawal from the distractions of the material world as a pre-requisite for the adoration of the Deity. Although it was eventually more or less subsumed by the dogma and ritual of the Roman Church, that impulse has been carried down the centuries and still, in slightly modified form, underpins worship in Celtic lands, even today.

Chapter 2

AIDAN

On the remote and isolated Magilligan Peninsula on Ireland's North Derry coast, a small cairn of stones marks the resting place of certain of the bones of 'the Blessed Aidan'. At the same time, other bones of the saint lie in a tomb at the Abbey of Lindisfarne, whilst other relics are reputed to be held at Glastonbury. Who was Aidan and how did his body come to eventually reside in so many different places? The answer is a rather complex one.

Virtually nothing is known of Aidan's early life except that he was Irish. Our only real source concerning him is the Venerable Bede (AD 673–735) who recounts his life after he came to England but nothing before that. Legends say that he was of noble blood, from the Dal Cassian lineage of the Kingdom of Thomond (parts of Counties Clare and Galway), that he was somehow related to St. Brigid of Kildare and that he had served some time in a religious community on Scattery Island, just off the coast of Co. Clare. However, much of this is simply folktale, added long after Aidan's death.

It is thought that Aidan came to the kingdom of Bernica in Northern England around the year 635, in the wake of King Oswald who had become a Christian during an enforced exile on the holy island of Iona. Oswald had regained his former throne by driving out Mercian invaders and was now anxious to establish a Christian kingship in the country. He looked to Iona for help in converting his countrymen who were, for the most part, pagan. In reply, the abbey on Iona sent him a severe unnamed monk who returned to the foundation almost immediately complaining that the Saxons of the north were too ungodly and unteachable to be converted. He was replaced by Aidan who was a recent arrival on Iona but was already highly regarded for his piety, discretion and prudence. Aidan had the full blessing of the Ionian abbot Seghen and was allegedly consecrated as a bishop. Oswald gave the new holy man the island of Lindisfarne upon which to build an abbey that would serve him as a base from which he could begin his work across the country. The island was close to the royal palace at Bamburgh and provided a powerful political link between Church and throne. Aidan accepted the gift in preference to the then vacant see of York, which was further away from the royal power-base. It may also have been due to the fact that York had strong connections with Rome whereas Aidan may have had much closer ties to the Celtic church of Iona. The spreading of the Gospel in the southern part of Oswald's domain – the kingdom of Deria – was left to Paulinus 'the Blessed Aidan's evangel' with Aidan himself concentrating his efforts in the northern realm.

The relationship between Aidan and Oswald certainly seems to have been a particularly close one. Aidan is believed to have spoken only Irish and Oswald, who spoke the tongue, acted as translator into the Bernican language. There may also have been hints at some kind of political collusion here for, tradition states that Aidan: 'spoke the Irish tongue when it pleased him and the king translated as he thought best' – hinting that Oswald could actually translate the saint's words as he saw fit. Nevertheless, under Oswald's patronage, Aidan founded many monasteries and a school for slave boys. It was a widespread custom amongst the Saxons to sell some of their children into slavery and Aidan set about educating such offspring. He believed that women should not be denied the opportunity of the religious life (a view not wholly shared by the Roman Church) and made St. Hilda, the daughter of Edwin of Northumbria, abbess of a convent in Hartlepool.

The monasticism which Aidan brought to the north of England closely followed that of the Irish system with which the saint was familiar and for a while, Aidan relied on monks from both Ireland and Scotland to populate the holy houses. Gradually however, his monasteries became self-sufficient and strongly independent and amongst Aidan's pupils were such well-known English saints as Wilfred of Hexham, Baoisil (Basil) of Melrose and Chad of Lichfield. His discipline was rigorous and monastic life consisted of prayer and fasting, coupled with long periods of meditation. Aidan himself lived in absolute poverty, which gave him the moral authority to frequently criticize the lifestyles of the wealthy and powerful all around him. This did not sit well in some quarters but it generated an aura of holy simplicity around Aidan's name in the common mind.

Although Aidan is said to have lived a frugal life, he did attend several large feasts that Oswald gave. At one of these, according to legend, the saint instructed the king to break up the silver dishes of the banquet and distribute them to destitute people who were clamouring at the Royal gates. Oswald did this, distributing some of the broken silver himself, and Aidan, grabbing the monarch's right arm, declared: 'May this kind hand never perish'. The Venerable Bede relates that after Oswald's death, his right hand remained supernaturally uncorrupted.

Oswald died in the year 642 and was succeeded by Oswin, with whom Aidan also enjoyed a good relationship. The new king presented the holy man with an exceptionally fine horse, which Aidan immediately gave away to a poor man. A horse was a symbol of rank since only the rich could ride but Aidan walked everywhere stating that he was 'amongst the most lowly of God's creatures'.

The times were, however, extremely turbulent and Oswin's kingship was not wholly secure. It was Aidan's custom to retire for the royal court on occasion for a period of meditation and reflection. In 651, he retreated to the Inner Farne island for a period of study and from there, it is said, he saw the town of Bamburgh, the Royal Seat, go up in flames under the attack of Penda, the militant king of Mercia. The war-like Mercian king instructed most of the outer house of the town to be pulled down and their wood to be piled up around the base of the stronghold. Then the Mercians waited for a favourable wind. In response to the prayers of the holy Aidan, the wind is said to have changed and the majority of the town was spared.

It is said that Aidan foresaw the death of Oswin at the hands of his nephew and successor Oswin. The royal line of Bernica was a notoriously unstable one, perhaps due to the fact that the kingdom was divided into two. Bernica stretched through present-day Northumberland and into south-east Scotland, whilst the southern portion (known as Deria) encompassed North Yorkshire and part of County Durham. Oswin ruled the southern end of the kingdom with Oswin ruling the northern end. The growing threat of Penda and his Mercians convinced Oswin that the whole kingdom should be united and he was determined to make war on his uncle to accomplish this. He eventually invaded Oswin's territory. Whether gifted with political foresight or whether granted a supernatural vision, Aidan foretold his benefactor's death, which he said, would be 'at the yhands of a kinsman and through grossest betrayal'. As Oswin's army advanced, Oswin fled the country to the relative protection of a neighbouring noble. It was an unfortunate move for he was betrayed and perished at the hand of his own nephew, just as Aidan had foretold. Although Oswin went on to the unite Bernica, the death of Oswin proved the end for the holy man of Lindisfarne.

The news of the murder gravely shocked Aidan. He had

been friendly to both supposedly Christian kings but had been especially close to Oswin. It is said that, at the time, he was not in good health and that the awful event actually hastened his death. Twelve days afterward, he was taken seriously ill and died at Bamburgh on 31st August 651. A tent had been erected for him against the west wall of the church and he is said to have expired with his head resting against a wooden post or support, used to strengthen the wall. Later, when the church was destroyed by fire, this particular post was not burned at all. This post itself later became an object of veneration and many pilgrimages came to Bamburgh in order to see it. Aidan's bones were buried in the cemetery at Lindisfarne but were later translated into the church itself.

In the year 664, the great Synod of Whitby took place, which more or less united the Celtic Church with that of Rome, and with the latter having dominance. Roman dogma began to take precedence over the more flexible and mystical Celtic ethos and, in some respects; the underlying ethos and structure of the Church were changed. Many of the Celtic abbots were not wholly in favour of the union, particularly as Roman bishops would be placed over them. One of these was Aidan's successor at Lindisfarne, St. Colman. Refusing the authority of the bishops, he took several of Aidan's bones and set sail for Ireland to establish a purely Celtic monastery. 'The Blessed Aidan should not lie in Roman soil,' he thundered. At Magilligan on the North Irish coast, he deposited the bones as a Celtic shrine for Irish pilgrims who espoused the Celtic Church and there they remain until this day. Colman and his followers went on to establish a short-lived Celtic foundation on the island of Inishbofin, off the coast of Co. Mayo.

In the year 793, the abbey of Lindisfarne was attacked and sacked by the Vikings and afterward Aidan's memory was somewhat eclipsed by that of his disciple Cuthbert. More of his bones were removed; some were placed in

Cuthbert's coffin and some reputedly taken to the island of Iona where Aidan had allegedly been a scholar. Further relics of the saint were removed to Glastonbury where the monks claimed a special affinity with Aidan. It was here that his feast-day – 31st August – was rigorously maintained. It was through the influence of the Glastonbury monks that Aidan's feast appears in the Wessex Calendars, which demonstrate the continuance of his cult after the age of Bede. They quaintly describe his Feast Day simply as 'Aidan's Rest'.

Bede himself wrote more kindly of Aidan than of any other saint although there were theological differences between the two men (Bede, for example, did not approve of Aidan's methods for calculating the date of Easter). He praised the saint for his piety and for his devout love of prayer, speaking warmly of his humility and of his willingness to help the sick and impoverished. He further contrasted Aidan's simplicity of faith with that of many of the bishops of his own time, holding the holy man up as an example of true Christianity.

Although the memory of Aidan was allowed to lapse slightly for many centuries after his death and he is not now regarded as one of the foremost Celtic saints, there is no doubt that he had a tremendous influence upon the establishment of the Church in England and upon those who came after him. A persistent Christian legend says that the young St. Cuthbert, whilst tending sheep in the Lammermuir Hills, saw the soul of Aidan, surrounded with supernatural light and escorted by cohorts of angels, ascend into Heaven at the moment of his death. Holy lights and music reverberated all through the mountains and Cuthbert himself was thrown down 'by the power of God'. This vision was to have a profound effect on the young boy and is said to have guided him towards the religious life. He was to become almost an influential a figure as Aidan himself had been. The example of Aidan, the simple monk, was carried down through the years as late as the Victorian era when the saint enjoyed a slight revival mainly due to J.B. Lightfoot, the Bishop of Durham who described him as the 'true Apostle of England'. And, above Magilligan Strand, close to a mid-19th century church, which bears his name, is a holy well consecrated to him and the cairn that marks his bones, bother tangible reminders of one of England's holiest of saints.

Chapter 3

BRIDGET

Although many of the early saints were male, there is no doubt that women also played an influential role in the development of the Celtic Church. Foremost amongst the names of the female saints is that of Bridget or Brigid, an Irish woman who lived in the late 5th and early 6th centuries. However, historical evidence about her is so scant there have even been questions as to whether she existed or not.

There are many stories as to Bridget's origin and of her birthplace but no one is really sure as to where in Ireland she was born. Some folkloric sources confidently assert that she was born in Co. Louth, at Faughart, near Dundalk and that she was the daughter of a druid (a pagan priest). Her name at this time was Brighde, which was the name of an ancient Celtic mother-goddess, widely worshipped amongst the pagans. This was later Anglicized into Bridget. Other tales state that she was born at Uinmeras, about 5 miles from present-day Kildare and that her parents were simple labouring folk. But no one is exactly sure about her birthplace or parentage. Nor does anyone know how she became a Christian or as to who baptized her. Certain sources say that she was born during the time of St. Patrick's ministry in Ireland and it was the saint himself who baptized her; others say that it was St. Ibar (Ibor), a holy man who operated a mission station in Louth who performed the sacred deed. One popular legend tells how Ibar, who was supposedly blessed with the supernatural power of prophesy, told his congregation that the Virgin Mary would appear amongst them on a certain day. A large crowd turned out to see this miraculous event and in the middle of them, Bridget wandered up to the very front. Setting eyes upon her, Ibar declared that the prophesy had been fulfilled and that this was indeed 'Mary of the Gael', the living embodiment of the Virgin. This was a name that remained with Bridget throughout her life. She further seemed to fulfill Ibar's prophesy by preaching most eloquently to the congregation on Christian themes, confirming herself as one of the future saints of Ireland.

There may also have been some truth in the tradition that she was raised in a Druid House for Bridget displayed a deep knowledge of ancient ways and beliefs. Amongst the druids – as in the early Celtic church – women were treated with equal respect as men and were educated to the same extent in the traditional forms of Irish culture. This knowledge stood Bridget in good stead when dealing with the pagan chieftains of the country. After being baptized by St. Ibar, Bridget is said to have returned home to look after her mother who was blind but later her father chose a marriage-partner for her, someone whom he considered suitable. Arranged marriages were not unusual in Celtic Ireland and were usually considered to increase the power, property and prestige of certain families. Bridget herself, who was seemingly twelve years old at the time, seemed to have had little say in the matter. However, when it came to the marriage itself, she refused to go through with it, even though her betrothed was a bard of some standing in Ireland (Bards or poets were considered to enjoy almost as high a status as a chieftain in ancient Ireland). Angered by her disobedience, her father drove her out of his house and Bridget went to dwell in a nearby convent. It is said that she received her nun's veil from the hand of St. Mel at Ardagh in Co. Longford where there is now a convent farm, known as St. Bridget's Training Centre. She was such an adept pupil that eventually she left the convent and returned to study with Ibar himself who actually is said to have consecrated her as a bishop. This is rather improbable and may have been added to her tale much later to grant her cult equal status with those of Patrick and Columcille.

Bridget did not live in seclusion as many of the other Celtic saints did but rather became a familiar figure around Kildare where she appears to have been friendly with many people. In fact, she seems to have been a charismatic figure around the Curragh where she lived at the time and where the Irish kings raised their horses. She is also said to have traveled widely around Ireland, concerning herself with local issues such as the treatment of captives by the various local kings and in the distributing of alms to the poor. Tradition states that she had a generous nature and that she was unstinting in the gifts which she gave and in the miracles that she performed. For instance, she is supposed to have given away her father's valuable sword to a leper whom she met upon the road and that she gave the food of her convent to beggars at the expense of the sisters there. Another story tells of how she cured another leper using water from a well that she'd blessed but when the cured man refused to show charity to another leper, she caused the disease to return to him. She is also credited with miracles regarding restoring the faculties of the dumb and the blind and various wells and bushes dedicated to her are dotted all across Ireland – all with healing properties. However, no historical record exists of her travels exists – much of the tradition comes from no earlier than the 8th century after Bridget had been dead for 100 – and it is possible that these stories are no more than folktales generated to give greater credit to a female saint.

Bridget's first foundation was said to have been at Drumcree, Co. Kildare. This monastic settlement was on a broad flood plain of the River Liffey and was upon land

supposedly granted to Bridget by the King of Lrinster himself, a recent convert to Christianity. The name 'Drumcree'
simply means the 'ridge of clay' and it was reputedly this
small foundation, which later increased immensely over
the years, which gave the Co. its name – 'Kildare' means
'church of the oak'. The name may have hinted at Bridget's
supposedly druidic origins for most of the churches which
were dedicated to her were close to oak trees and oak had
been a symbol of the pagan druid religion. One of those
who came to minister at the church was a Christian named
Conleth (or Conleith) who rose rapidly through the ranks
to become the first abbot-bishop of the foundation. Kildare
was a dual monastery – allegedly the first of its kind in the
country – in which monks and nuns lived side by side.
Conleth, who was a skilled metalworker, made great im-
provements to the church and is said to have sculpted an
elaborate crozier for her. This is now in the Royal Irish
Academy museum in Dublin. Nothing remains of either
the church or the foundation except for a round tower, probably added around the 8th or 9th centuries.

There are many miracles supposedly performed by St.
Brigit, especially concerning food and drink. As a young
girl, she is said to have distributed all of her mother's but-
ter, milk and meat to the poor going past her door, then
realizing that the family would have no food for themselves,
she prayed and the larder was miraculously replenished.
On another occasion she is said to have gathered with her
disciples on the shores of Lough Melvin in Co. Fermanagh
and to have surreptitiously consumed chicken with them
during Lent. Hearing that St. Patrick was on his way, she
prayed over the forbidden food, which was miraculously
transformed into fish (a permissible foodstuff during the
Lenten period). Since then, the flesh of all trout caught in
the Lough is said to taste of chicken.

As with her birth, no one is altogether sure of the date of
Bridget's death but it is thought to have been around AD 520

or (more likely) 525. It is reported that she was buried in a heavily ornamented casket studded with precious stones, denoting the status in which she was now held as Abbess of Kildare. This may simply be another legend as no trace of her casket has ever been found – it was supposed to have been moved from Kildare to either Armagh or Downpatrick sometime during the 9th or 10th centuries to avoid Viking raids along the Liffey and to lie with the bones of St. Patrick. Various *Lives* were subsequently written, including that by Cogitosus (supposedly written around AD 650 but most of these give little history concerning Bridget and rely mainly on folklore and fanciful tale. Although she is credited with the foundation of many churches throughout Ireland, it is now clear that the majority of these were established long after Bridget was already dead.

Although he life is certainly in question, there can be no doubt about the extension of her cult, particularly in Ireland and in the Irish-based churches on the Continent. No other saint, except Patrick, seems to have had more influence amongst the Irish Christians and Irish foundations. Translations of the *Lives* were made into English, Welsh, Old French and German and churches all over both the Celtic and Saxon worlds were dedicated to her. In England there were at least nineteen in her honour – the most famous being St. Bride's in Fleet Street, London. There were other foundations in Wales, the most celebrated at St. Bride's Bay in Dafyd – indeed it's thought that her cult was almost as strong in Wales as it was in Ireland. She is also venerated in Alsace, Flanders and Portugal. In Lisbon it is claimed that the saint's skull was venerated in the nearby town of Lumiar where it was carried from Ireland by several Irish knights en route to the Crusades around 1280. No trace of the shrine remains today but Bridget herself in highly respected all across the Portuguese countryside.

Even in death, Bridget remained controversial concerning her roots with pagan Ireland. Gerald of Wales (scribe and confessor to King John) writing in the 12th century re-lates of how a perpetual fire was kept burning inside an enclosure, thickly encircled by bushes in Kildare, which was tended by twenty nuns. This strongly associated her with a fire-cult which is supposed to have flourished on the plains of Kildare and whose goddess Brig, whose name meant 'valour' or 'might' had her feast on 1st February, which later became St. Bridget's Day. Another connection with her supposedly pagan past was the St. Bridget's Cross, usually woven from reeds or rushes which bears more of a relation to the Swastika (an ancient pagan symbol) than the Christian Cross and is said to be far older that Chris-tianity. These are usually hung above the door on St. Bridget's Eve (31st January) to ensure good luck to a house-hold for the coming year. Such artifacts have overtones of pagan magic about them and are not officially sanctioned by the Church.

St. Bridget was adopted as the patron saint of blacksmiths and of all those who work in metal. This may have come about through her close association with Conleth who was said to have been 'very skilled in the workings of metal'. For obvious reasons too, she also became the patron saint of Irish healers. During childbirth in the Western Isles of Scotland, particularly in Uist, the *bean ghluine* (knee women – local midwives) would call on the name of Bridget as they assisted women in labour. This was justified by the mythi-cal tale that Bridget herself had acted as midwife at the birth of Jesus in Bethlehem and that she had soothed the Virgin's brow with the hem of her robe. Therefore she was the one to call upon for aid and comfort at the birth of a child. In Ireland, she is also considered to be the patron saint of poets and writers.

The only real relic of Bridget – her cloak – was donated by Gunhilda, sister of the Saxon King Harold II to the ab-bey of St. Donatian in Bruges, Belgium in 1087. Harold had fled to Belgium and had been given sanctuary there and so the abbey was accorded the right to hold this relic of the saint in perpetuity.

Bridget may have been a controversial saint and her very existence may have been called into question but there is no doubt that she has left a lasting legacy, both in Ireland and far beyond.

Chapter 4

COLUMBA/COLUMCILLE

Arguably no saint is more controversial that Columcille (known in Scotland as Columba), since he started a bloody war, was forced to abandon his native Ireland for Scotland, was despised by some of his contemporaries and yet was one of the foremost saints within the Celtic Church. In fact in was Columcille who founded what was to become the centre of the Celtic form of Christianity – the monastic establishment on the island of Iona.

Although the name Columcille means 'dove of the church', it's owner was not so meek or peaceful – on the surface at least. Irascible, even spiteful and conscious of his status, he dominated both the Irish and Scots ecclesiastical orders during his lifetime and laid the foundations for Celtic worship after he was gone.

Columcille was born into a Royal Irish family – the Ui Niall (O'Neil) – at Lough Gartan, Donegal in AD 563. Legend states that the birth was foretold many years before my Mochta, a disciple of St. Patrick, who correctly predicted that Columcille would be born on Thursday 7th December. This gave rise to the old but widespread Irish belief that Thursdays were the best days to start any new undertaking, as it will have been blessed by the saint. His birth-name was Crimthan meaning 'cunning wolf' or 'fox' and he could trace his lineage back to a celebrated High King of Ireland, Niall of the Nine Hostages. As a prince of the family, he could have been (theoretically at least) a contender for the

High Kingship of Ireland himself, however he chose the Church instead. As a young boy, he was frequently to be found in prayer giving him the nickname 'Columcille' – Columba in its Latinised form. Nevertheless, there were in his character, still some traces of the old secular pride in his princely status and this was to later prove his undoing. Columcille was trained as a monk, first by Finnian of Movilla in Co. Down and then by Finnian of Clannard in Meath. From the former and from a bard named Master Gemnan, he was to learn his love of music and poetry, from the latter, he was to gain great scholarship and understanding. From Clonard, he traveled to Glasnevin in Dublin where he was ordained by St. Mobhi.

It is said that whilst studying at Cloanrd, an angel appeared to him and offered him two holy gifts of his own choosing. Columcille chose chastity and wisdom and a third gift of prophecy was added as well. He also have seems to have had a great talent for poetry and some of his alleged manuscripts are preserved in the Bodleian Library, Oxford. Three Latin poems, including the *Altus Prosator* may very well be his own composition.

At the age of only twenty-five, he founded his first monastery in the year 546. This was on an extremely pagan site – a druid oak grove name Doire Calgach, which was renamed Doire Cholm Cille in the saint's honour. The new site has stood for over 1,000 years and is now the city of Derry, Northern Ireland's second city. However, there is no trace of the monastery which he founded. Although it was Derry which remained close to his heart, ten years later, Columcille was to found yet another monastery at Durrow in Co. Offaly and may have been the possible founder of Kells in Co. Meath and Moone in Co. Kildare.

Besides a talent for music and poetry, Columcille seems to have had great skill as a copyist and illustrator and he is recorded as having produced a number of books in his own hand. One is a collection of Psalms known as the 'Cathach' or Battle Book of the O'Donnells – a clan with whom he shared ancestry – because it was later carried into battle in front of that family. Reputedly, Columcille produced between 300–400 handwritten books in his lifetime and though this is clearly an exaggeration, it shows the love that the saint had for books and book learning. So great was his love of poetry, history and tradition that he was also fond of finding and transcribing very ancient texts. For example, he is believed to have led a party of pilgrims to the tomb of St. Martin of Tours and unearthed an ancient volume – supposedly over 100 years old – which had lain on St. Martin's breast. Whether or not he desecrated the tomb site to retrieve it is unknown but he was criticized by other churchmen for his 'theft, not that he seems to have paid much attention to their censure. It was this alleged arrogance that was to seriously jeopardize his ministry in Ireland.

In the year 561, Columcille returned to the monastery at Movilla to visit his former mentor Finian. He was about forty years old at the time. The foundation houses an ancient manuscript known as St. Martins Gospel, which was supposed to be a compilation of the first four Synoptic Gospels, together with a condensation of the Mosaic Law. The text was a Latin translation of an even older work, compiled by St. Jerome, which Fiaian had copied at the Scottish foundation at Whithorn from a work, which St. Ninian had brought from Gaul. It was a work of great antiquity and importance.

Columcille was extremely jealous of his former teacher because of the ownership of the volume and whilst Finian and his monks were asleep, he began to make a copy of it each night. He was, however, soon discovered. Finian was enraged and demanded that the duplicated book should be handed over to him for retention at his monastery. Columcille refused saying that the matter should be placed in front of the Irish High King Dairmid for a judgment.

After listening to both sides, Dairmid gave the first recorded copyright judgment: 'To every cow its calf and to ever book its copy'. Columcille's copy should be handed over to Finian. It was now Columcille's turn to be enraged. He refused to accept the ruling and called on his kinsmen to make war on the High King. It was a spiteful and irresponsible call but the Ui Niall answered it and Dairmid was forced to confront them.

The armies met in the alley of Cuildrevne in Co. Sligo and many thousands of soldiers were killed in bloody slaughter. Even Columcille was appalled when he heard of the carnage. Diarmid was defeated but appealed immediately to the church authorities to deal with Columcille and the death that he'd caused. The matter was taken extremely seriously and a Synod was convened at Teltown, Co. Meath to discuss what action should be taken. The Synod decided that Columcille should be excommunicated and denied all rights of the church. However, his friend Brendan of Birr came to his defence and succeeded in overturning the decision but the honour of the High King was still not satisfied. He demanded that Columcille should be severely punished for the bloodshed he had caused.

Columcille himself had fled to the hermitage of his old friend St. Molaise on Devenish Island in Lough Erne, Co. Fermanagh. It was said that Molaise was afflicted by terrible diseases, but that his word was respected by the Synod of Teltown. It was Molaise who imposed the penance, which the Synod ratified – a lifetime exile from his native Ireland, to go as a missionary to win as many souls for Christ as had been lost in battle. For a proud and arrogant Irish prince, it was a harsh sentence but in the year 565, he sailed away from Ireland for good, taking with him twelve apostles. He had vowed never to see or set foot in Ireland again.

Their first landfall was on the island of Oronsay in the Inner Hebrides but Columcille found that from here he could still see the Irish coastline, the sight of which he claimed, would cause him great pain. So they continued their voyage, heading northward, eventually landing on the island of Hu or Hy. The island had been a central one in pagan worship and contained two major shrines – one to Lugh, the Celtic god of light and one 60 Shony, a sea deity. There was also an important cemetery here known as Relig Odhrain, in which the kings of Irish Dalriada (which stretched between the north of Ireland and Scotland) were buried. A small church, founded by Columcille's cousin, Odhran of Latteragh also stood on Hu and it was close to this, now well out of sight of Ireland, that the voyagers founded a monastery. Columcille changed the name of the island from Hu to Iona (it had been previously also known as I-Shony in honour of the sea god). At the same time he changed his own name from Columcille to Columba, the name by which he is known in Scotland.

The monastry on Iona was now Columba's principal foundation from which his monks traveled on missionary journeys, chiefly into Scotland. His most famous mission was to the Pictish kingdoms of the Scottish north ruled over by Brude mac Beli in the year 574. Before he arrived at Brude's court, legend says, Columba save the life of a man who was being threatened by a mighty creature from a lake. The saint made the sign of the Cross and the creature fled. This is reputed to be one of the earliest sightings of the Lough Ness Monster! Brude, however, refused the missionaries admission to his stronghold, locking the gates against them. However, Columba simply made the sign of the Cross once more and they swung open. The astonished king and his subjects immediately accepted Christianity; and Brude was instrumental in securing the tenure of Iona for the community there.

Although he had vowed that he would not see Ireland again nor set foot on its soil, Columba did in fact return once – this was for the Council of Drumcatt (Druim-Cetta), which took place in AD 580. The exact location of the Council is uncertain but it is thought to have been somewhere near present-day Limavady in Co. Derry (although Ballycastle in Co. Antrim also claims it). According to tradition, he attended the Council blindfold and with sods of Scottish earth tied to his feet so that he would not break his vow. The Council had originally been called by the Irish High King to discuss the problem of bards and fili (genealogical rhymers) who had been critical of his reign. Fearful of their position, the poets called on the saint to come and represent them. Columba arrived and proceeded to introduce other issues into the Council – the position of women in the Irish army, the obligations of the Irish in Scotland to the Irish High King – until the Council broke up, indecisive on the original issue. It was an ancient example of filibustering.

About four years before his death, Columba's health began to fail and he more or less withdrew from active holy life, spending much of his time transcribing books. However his approaching demise was both foreseen and sensed even, says his biographer Adamnan, by his favourite horse, which reputedly wept tears when he stroked its head during his last day on earth. He had spent part of the night copying the Psalms but just before morning laid his pen aside, declaring that someone else could finish the work. It was the 9th June 597 and it was the same year that St. Augustine arrived from Rome and landed in Kent. Before Matins, he was dead.

The monastery that he'd founded, however, lived on and grew in importance within the Celtic church – in fact, becoming its very centre. His influence, through the founding of other monastic houses in both Ireland and Scotland was considerable. In fact, for many years after his death, he was widely considered to be the patron saint of Scotland long before St. Andrew (although Andrews relics had been brought to Scotland by St. Rule, the saint was still considered to be a Palestinian as opposed to Columba's Celtic birth). Following repeated Viking raids on Iona, the saint's relics were moved to Dunkeld where they became an object of pilgrimage. The first, best-known biography of the saint was written about one hundred years after his death by Adamnan, one of his successors as Abbot of Iona, who comprehensively describes the miracles, prophesies and visions attributed to the saint. His Feast Day is given in the medieval calendars as 9th June.

From the biography, Columcille/Columba emerges as a tall, powerful and imposing figure, of muscular build and with an impressive presence; a man of unique vision and an able scholar who has left an indelible impression upon the church of which he was a part and upon Christianity down through the ages.

Chapter 5

COLUMBANUS

Sometimes confused, because of his name, with his contemporary St. Columba (Columcille), St. Columbanus was, nevertheless, instrumental in carrying the Celtic church to continental Europe. Like Columba, he left behind a number of writings. Whilst these are mainly letters, there is also a Penitential as well as several poems, one of which (a boating song) is his most famous. Through these, we know slightly more about him than we do of some other saints.

Columbanus was born in the Kingdom of Leinster in Ireland, possibly around AD 543, and probably (as with many other Celtic saints) of a noble and wealthy family. His entry into the Church was foretold by a local woman hermit – and whilst his mother was firmly against this, it soon became clear that this was what the child wished to do. By all accounts, he was an extremely good looking young man and he foreswore any female friendships in order to remain chaste and suitable for the holy life. He was educated at a small monastic school at Killeigh in Co. Offaly, before proceeding to study at the great abbey of Bangor in Co. Down. His first teacher, tradition states was a monk named Sinall, a disciple of St. Finnan, who helped the young novice to overcome carnal temptation but his later instructor was St. Comgall, the influential abbot of Bangor. Columbanus proved himself to be a bright, intelligent and willing pupil and seemed from the outset to be destined for great things. He was ordained a priest in the year 572. He stayed on with Comgall for a good number of years but then set out, with eleven companions (as was the Celtic custom) to found new holy houses in France. He stated that he had 'chosen voluntary exile for Christ'.

They settled first in Burgundy, which at that time was wild and untamed country, and here the monks had to survive on wild roots and herbs. They moved on to Annegray where Columbanus established his first religious foundation. The monastery at Annegray was founded in the ruins of a former Roman fort, which had been given to him by King Childedbert II of Austrasia, and Columbanus' preaching soon drew numerous followers to the area. Moving on, Columbanus and his followers founded a further monastery at Luxeuil and another at Fontaines. All three holy houses were widely renowned for their learning and also for their illuminated copies of the Gospels. The quality of the work from Luxieul in particular became well known all across France. All three monasteries followed what was called 'the Irish tradition', keeping the Irish (Celtic) date for Easter, having a bishop who was subservient to an abbot and using Irish penitential practices. These varied in tone and practice from the surrounding Frankish monasteries, and friction was inevitable.

Confrontation occurred with the death of Childebert with various neighbouring monasteries attacking both the practices of his monks, his date for Easter and Columbanus personally. His loyalty to Rome was called into question and he was forced to write directly to Pope Gregory I (Gregory the Great: AD 590–604) and later to one of his successors Boniface IV (AD 608–615) assuring both pontiffs of the fealty of his foundations but at the same time steadfastly maintaining that the Celtic church upheld very ancient traditions of Christianity which had remained unsullied from earliest times. However, this did not appease his enemies and several years later, he was openly attacked by the Archbishop of Lyons and was forced, once again, to write to the

Synod of Chalon, adopting a less strident tone and plead-
ing for toleration both for his monks and for himself. He
simply wished, he stated, to live according to the monastic
traditions of his native Ireland. Grudgingly, the Synod gave
its consent. But worse was to come for Columbanus.

Shortly after his plea to Chalon, King Theuderic II of
Burgundy called upon Columbanus to bless his four illegitimate sons so that one of them might take the throne
after his death. Adopting a high moral standpoint the saint
refused, loftily declaring 'None of these will ever hold the
scepter since they have been begotten in sin'. These were
unwise words for they draw down upon the saint not only
the anger of the king but also of the queen-grandmother
Brunhild. Theuderic ordered that Columbanus and his
monks be deported back to Ireland and sent a military es-
cort to convey them to Nantes. Hardly had the ship left port,
when a fearful storm broke forcing it back to shelter.
Columbanus took this as a sign that he was not to leave the
Continent and so, disembarking, set out for the court of
King Clotar II of Neustria, moving on later to Metz in
Austrasia where at King Theudebert's court, he met up again
with some of the monks from Luxeuil.

After founding a number of smaller monasteries,
Columbanus moved on again. He and his followers traveled up the river Rhine and into modern-day Switzerland
as far as Lake Constance. Here one of his traveling companions, St. Gall, took ill and decided to rest. He founded
a small hermitage and the town and canton of St-Gall is
named after him. Columbanus and the others now planned
to found a monastery at Bregenz on the shores of the Lake
but they met with such fierce opposition that they were
forced to abandon the project. However, they remained in
the area. The region, however, was exceptionally turbulent and Columbanus was, once again, about to become the
victim of local politics.

Warfare raged between King Theudebert and King

Theuderic and his Burguindian forces; and the victory of the latter made the saint's position at Constance untenable (since Austrasia now a province of Burgundy). For eighteen months Columbanus and his monks had taken an uncompromising Christian position, smashing idols and disrupting pagan ceremonies. Theuderic was still pagan and relations between himself and Columbanus were still not good. Monks were being murdered in the woods and churches were mysteriously burned – doubtless on Theuderic's orders.

For the sake of his mission, the saint moved on once more. He crossed the Alps and into the Duchy of Lombardy, and area of Italy which had been settled by German tribes. Columbanus spent much of the year 613 in Milan, but traveled on again, eventually settling at Bobbio in the Apennines.

He was now an old man – over 70 years of age – and he was tired of traveling. This area was ruled over by the Arian Duke Agilof (Agiluf) whose wife, Queen Theudelina and sons were Catholics. However, they had been separated from Rome by the vexed doctrinal question of the Three Chapters (the writings of Theodore of Mopsuestia; certain writings of Theodoret of Cyrus and the letter of Ibas to Maris). Agilof wished to be reconciled with Rome and so he was reasonably tolerant of Columbanus and his monks. The saint wrote directly to the Roman ecclesiastical authorities on the king's behalf outlining the monarch's views in a simple but eloquent way and a measure of reconciliation was affected.

In return, Agilof granted Columbanus and his brothers some property in the area of Bobbio, which contained little more than a stretch of rough land and a ruined church. Nevertheless from this, at the end of the year 613., the saint established yet another monastic foundation and he is said to have taken an active part in its actual construction. This was to become Columbanus' most important holy house.

Bobbio was to become one of the most famous monasteries in Europe, renowned for its learning and for its celebrated library. After all the years of traveling Columbanus eventually settled there and enjoyed the status as a holy man which was now accorded to him. He was now a very old man and allegedly very frail. However, his Rule at Bobbio was a strict and rather severe one. Like his other foundations, the Rule there followed that of the Irish monasteries, which was both strict and demanding. Even novices were supposed to wear horsehair shirts, to subsist largely on roots and wild herbs (Feast Days were an exception) and to sometimes pray whilst standing in a river or pond of freezing water. And the Rule of Columbanus was rigorously enforced and those who broke it were corporally and publicly punished. The emphasis was on prayer, work and study. Bobbio was not a place for the faint hearted.

Even so, St. Columbanus emerges as saintly, although a slightly man. On matters of faith, morality and discipline he was particularly uncompromising. And he seems to have been largely intolerant of the sin – particularly the carnal sin –, which characterized his own time. And yet he had his gentle side. He enjoyed closeness with nature. His biographer Jonas (one of his followers) tells us of how even the wildest animals came to lick his hands as he passed. And the saint seemed to have a miraculous power over beasts and a sense of 'oneness' with the natural world. According to Jonas birds, especially robins nested and raised their young within his cowl whilst squirrels and doves played amongst the folds of his robes. Both trees and bushes flourished and died at his command and fish in rivers and lakes came at his call. He emerges as a man of many contrasts – stern yet gentle, impassive in matters of faith, yet loving and sensitive in matters of nature. Even into his final years, it is said, he still remained very attractive to women.

Columbanus died at Bobbio on 21st November in the year

615 (some calendars give the 23rd November) and his remains still rest within the modern church there. The monastery he had built developed and flourished and the de-
lightful town of San Columbano was named after its
founder. Monks from all over the Christian world came to
Bobbio to study and its fame spread far and wide. It's learning, its vast library and its precious collection of insular
manuscripts, were the envy of the monastic world. The
Rule of Columbanus, though certainly influential in monastic circles was too severe for some, particularly the element of corporal punishment in the case of disobedience.
Shortly after the saint's death it was largely replaced by
the Rule of St. Benedict, which although in many ways
just as strict, was more amenable to the spiritual life there.
Despite this, Columbanus was still held up as an example
of excellence in inspiration and as a promoter of pioneering achievements.

Sensing that his end was near, Columbanus' thoughts
turned to his thoughts to his friend St. Gall who had been
with him since his days in Bangor. In the last years, there
had been an estrangement between the two men, which
had saddened Columbanus. Gall was still alive and living
in a hermitage, an itinerant preacher in the Tuggen area
around Lake Zurich, and on his deathbed in Bobbio, the
saint gave strict orders that his holy staff be sent to his
former colleague. He also named Gall as his successor as
abbot. It is not known as to whether Gall accepted the holy
staff but he certainly did not accept the abbotship. The disagreements between the two men were evidently too deep
and though the monks offered him the abbotship of one of
the best-known monasteries in Europe, St. Gall refused
preferring to end his days as a traveling preacher. Some
sources say, however, that Gall accepted the staff and kept
it by him until his own death in the year 630.

The main artistic representation of St. Columbanus is, however not in Bobbio at all but in one of the other monasteries

which he founded at Fontaines. He is standing, a severe but Godly man, holding an open scroll which reads:

'He sought a place and built another monastery, which he named Fontaines'

In the turbulent world of 7th century continental Europe, St. Columbanus stands out surely as one of Ireland's greatest apostles and missionaries: a saint who, at great personal danger, brought the word of Celtic Christianity to the warring, pagan countries of Europe. His influence has lived on to the present through the work of the monasteries that he founded. It is a fitting tribute to the holy man from Leinster.

Chapter 6

CUTHBERT

On the 31st August, AD 651, a young boy tending sheep, looked up as night descended over the Lammermuir Hills in northern England, to behold a wondrous sight. The sky was filled with a marvelous light that stretched out like a road, stretching from earth to Heaven, along which a procession of angels came and went, descending then returning. What the astonished shepherd had witnessed was the progression of the soul of the saintly Aidan, the holy bishop of Lindisfarne into Paradise. The sight had such an impact upon the boy, Cuthbert, that he resolved to turn immediately to the holy life and become a monk. Thus began the religious career of one of the North of England's most popular saints.

The above story is perhaps an embellished folktale but there is no doubt that the cult of St. Cuthbert was one of the most influential all through large part of England, Cornwall, Scotland and even the North of Ireland. And a little is known of the historical figure behind such a movement. Cuthbert was born into a large and relatively well-to-do Saxon family around AD 634. According to custom, both he and several siblings were fostered out to a woman called Kenswith and her husband who seem to have treated the young Cuthbert extremely well. Following his alleged vision in the Lammermuir Hills. Cuthbert presented himself at the great abbey of Melrose, late in 651, with the intention of taking holy orders. It is said that he was turned away and told to return a little later, as the lands around Melrose were in turmoil. Cuthbert went to train as a soldier but found military life not to his taste. He returned to Melrose where the prior is said to have viewed him from a window as he approached and instinctively uttered the words 'Behold the Servant of the Lord'.

Cuthbert seems to have struck up a close friendship with the prior of Melrose, Boisil and with the abbot Eata and when the latter moved on to Ripon to found a monastery there on estates given to him by Oswin of Bernica's son, King Alcfrith, Cuthbert moved with him. Alcfrith, however, placed a condition upon the new monastery – that it adopt Roman customs rather than the Celtic traditions of Melrose. This was too much for the Melrose monks who withdrew and Eata was succeeded as abbot of Ripon by St. Wilfred. Boisil died in AD 661, leaving Cuthbert as his named successor as Prior. The Priory was, however, under a rather grim prophecy. Before his death, Boisil had foretold that three years later, Melrose would be struck by a virulent 'yellow plague' (jaundice?), which would kill many of the Brethren. Eata and Cuthbert would, however, be spared but one would be considerably weakened by the passing of the disease. In 664, the prophecy came true as Melrose and the countryside round about was swept with a terrible fever. Many died and Cuthbert himself appeared to succumb to the pestilence but the monks prayed all night that he should be spared and eventually he was. The disease however had left its marked and for the rest of his life Cuthbert suffered from an internal disorder that left him physically weak and in great discomfort.

Nevertheless, this did not inhibit Cuthbert's missionary work and he traveled extensively between the coast of Berwickshire and Northumberland as far as the shores of the Solway Firth. Here the town of Kirkcudbright in Galloway is named after him. In all his travels and like many other Celtic saints, Cuthbert is supposed to have maintained a strong affinity with animal life. Indeed, it is said to have been local animals who kept him supplied with food on his journeys. One story is told of how an eagle dived into a river to capture a salmon in order to feed the saint and his companion. Cuthbert broke the fish in tow and shared it with the bird who had brought them their meal. Again, he is supposed to have been friendly towards otters, which he found along the banks of the rivers and these animals are said to have used their fur to dry the saint after he had bathed.

In 664, the great Synod of Whitby took place. Formally linking the Roman and Celtic churches. Following the Synod, Cuthbert accepted Roman practices and took over the great foundation at Lindisfarne which had been established by St. Aidan. There is no doubt that he was a saintly man and his gifts of healing were widely celebrated around the abbey and beyond but not all the monks were happy with his ready adoption of Roman practices. In order to engage in religious meditation and perhaps to escape criticism of his ways, Cuthbert withdrew for long periods to St. Cuthbert's Isle, just off the coast of Lindisfarne to live in recluse as a hermit. However, this did not prove sufficiently isolated for him and in 676 AD, he sought permission to travel to the Farne Islands further out to sea, which St. Aidan had also used as a retreat. He lived in a single stone cell with an adjoining oratory, sunk so far into the ground that no vision from land or see could distract him. Here he prayed and meditated whilst life continued at Lindisfarne. He had only the seabirds for company and perhaps this is one of the reasons that the Farne Islands were chosen as a bird sanctuary in the 20th century. They are now under the care and control of the National Trust. A special breed of eider duck which are known to breed there and settle along the Northumbrian coast are widely known as 'St. Cuthbert's Ducks'. He was also visited by ravens which, it is said, brought him strips of hog fat with which to grease his sandals.

Reports of Cuthbert's holiness spread far and wide across northern England and monks traveled from the abbey at

Bamburgh (also founded by St. Aidan) to visit him. He became known all through England as 'the Light of the North' and as one of the country's most sanctified men. Those who made it out to the remote Farne Island expressed surprised at how he managed to survive in this remote spot. The soil was scanty and poor and nothing would grow and so the story spread that he was fed by angels.

At the Synod of Twyford in 684, Cuthbert was elected by King and clergy to the see of Hexham and was invited to take up his new bishopric. Cuthbert refused, flatly stating that nothing would make him leave his island retreat. In reply, a fleet of boats, containing some of the greatest local noblemen and headed by the King himself, set sail for the Farnes to plead with the saint. At first Cuthbert refused their requests but he was also conscious of a prophesy issued by Prior Boisil before his death that once day he (Cuthbert) would be a bishop and in the end he complied and was consecrated at York on Easter Day – 26th March 685. However, he did not take up his new post but traveled to Lindisfarne where he stayed with his former companion Eata who was now bishop there.

From the monastery, he traveled back to his hermitage in the Farne Islands. The monks of Lindisfarne, on the instructions of their bishop, tried to visit him in his lonely seclusion but a series of storms prevented them from putting to sea. When they did arrive, Cuthbert's health had deteriorated considerably and they found that his entire food store consisted of five onions, only one of which had been slightly nibbled.

Shortly afterward. Cuthbert died, his demise signaled by the waving of two blazing torches, which were seen back at Lindisfarne. His body was carried back by boat and was buried in the church of St. Peter at Lindisfarne. Eleven years afterwards, his body was elevated to a shrine and was found to be totally uncorrupted, giving further proof of his saintliness.

In 875, Lindisfarne was attacked and almost completely destroyed by the Vikings. The shrine of the Blessed Cuthbert traveled around northern England and Southwest Scotland in order to avoid the Norsemen. It rested in such places as Ripon, Norham-on-Tweed and Chester-le-Street. Eventually they were placed behind the High Altar at Durham Cathedral, a final resting place for a much-loved saint.

The translation of his remains into the Cathedral was, however, not an easy one. They were hidden 'in the earth' to 'preserve them from the Danes' (Vikings) and a small Saxon church seems to have been built over them into which Cuthbert's relics were translated in 999 AD. Durham became a monastic site in 1083, due to the influence of William of St. Carilef and the neighbouring monasteries of Wearmouth and Jarrow were also restored. All these were, however, Anglo-Saxon in outlook but they still venerated a largely Celtic saint in the form of Cuthbert and so the remains were further translated into the new Norman Cathedral in 1104 when once again they were found to be uncorrupted. During the Reformation, they were again unearthed and inspected and once again found to be 'extremely life-like' in appearance. They were reburied in their original site until 1828 when they were exhumed once more and inspected. The remains were reburied but secondary relics such as vestment and a pectoral cross are now housed in the monastic buildings at Durham. There are a number of important manuscripts associated with Cuthbert – King Athelstan of Northumbria is supposed to have offered 96 pounds of silver, two Gospel books and a Life of the saint at the shrine which are now lodged in Corpus Christi College in Cambridge.

The cult of Cuthbert was already well known and was reasonably well established by the end of the 7th century but it was between the years 1000–1200 that it achieved its apogee. A number of *Lives* of the saint appeared and collections of miracle tales concerning Cuthbert began to circulate. He became the subject of the first fully illustrated *Life* of any saint – an extremely important work which is now held in University College, Oxford. One of the most influential accounts of his life was written by the Venerable Bede, which was much in demand on the Continent as well as in England. This spread the cult far wider than these island shores. There was an interest in his in Mainz in Germany where the bishop St. Lull, asked for and received a copy of Bede's account of Cuthbert's life By the middle of the 12th century, Reginald of Durham was able to proclaim that Cuthbert was one of the most popular saints in England and further afield. St. Cuthbert also appears in the iconography of the later Middle Ages and has a window in York Minister as well as paintings on the backs of stalls in Carlisle Cathedral.

From Durham, the cult spread itself out and its influence must have been formidable. Churches would appear to have been founded all across England, Scotland, Wales and Cornwall. Sites as far apart as Cotherstone in North Yorkshire and Cubert in south Cornwall reflect the spread of the cult and the saint's influence. The ruined church of Dunluce Castle, near Portrush in Co. Antrim, Northern Ireland (itself an important administrative centre) also bears his name. There are also many geographical features on the Inner Farne, where he spent his days as a religious hermit, which are dedicated to the saint. Indeed, the Inner Farne (where he had died) continued to be a place of retreat for the monks of Lindisfarne and for those from Durham for many years. A small hermitage was built there to accommodate them and this again was dedicated to St. Cuthbert.

Around the shores of Lindisfarne, it is still possible to find what are known locally as 'St. Cuthbert's beads' – the fossilized stems of crinoidal lilies, which in their stylized condition resemble the beads of a rosary. Even today Cuthbert can exert an influence on the imagination of Northern Christians.

Chapter 7

DAVID/DEWI

The austere and slightly forbidding figure known throughout Wales as Dewi Sant, or as Ddyfrwr (the Waterman), is
the only British holy man who was actually born in the country of which he is the patron saint. He is also the only Welsh
saint to have been canonized and having his own cult in
the Western Church. His influence was profound throughout the Celtic world stretching as far as Cornwall,
Herefordshire and Brittany. It is a great pity then that so
little is known about him.

It is thought that David was originally a saint of Dyfed
(Pembrokeshire) and that he lived around the 6th century,
the date of his death being given as either 589 or 601. Legend says that his birth was foretold, more than twenty or
thirty years before it occurred, by an angel who appeared
firstly to his father Sant, a scion of the royal house of
Ceredigion and then to several other saints including St.
Patrick. It is also said that angels ministered at his birth
when he mother Non was experiencing difficulties. These
fables are no more than products of a religious imagination. St. Patrick is supposed to have died sometime in the
5th century and could not therefore have been alive in the
6th when David most probably have been born and the
notion of a n Annunciation or foretelling may be an attempt
to link David's birth with that of Christ Himself. The names
Sant and Non-are quite simply Welsh variants of the words
'Saint' and 'Nun' which would seem to take away from any

veracity in the legend. Long before David was born, tradition goes on, his father had a dream in which an angelic voice told him that during his hunting trip the next day, he would chase and kill a stag near the River Teifi and in the same place as its body lay he would find a fish and a hive of bees. These would be tokens that would anticipate the life of his unborn son. It was believed that stags were a noble animal, which ate snakes and exemplified the victory of Christianity over the forces of evil. The hive of bees symbolized great wisdom and multiplicity of thought whilst the fish showed a sustained abstinence from strong drink, which was to give David his nickname of the Waterman (since he drank only water).

Sant, who was little more than a boy himself at this stage, paid no attention to the dream but continued to live a roisterous Royal life. David's mother Non was also of noble birth and was reputed to have been a great beauty. She was also modest and shy. One day whilst out hunting, Sant saw her and became inflamed with lust. He attacked and raped her, leaving her pregnant. In a dream, a local ruler received information that a child would be born in his country that would change all the kingdoms round about. He determined that he would kill this miraculous infant. However, before he could set out, a violent storm arose, keeping everyone indoors and unable to travel. All, that is, except Non, who made her way to a nearby ruined chapel, which boasted a holy, healing well both of which still bear her name. As she lay in labour, the storm raged around her but she was untouched by it. Angels came and ministered to her and a marvelous radiance protected her whilst she gave birth. Even after David was born, miracles continued to occur. A beautiful bush grew where the young child was laid and at his baptism, a blind monk who was holding him whilst he was being anointed had his sight restored. There was no doubt that David was a special child and was destined for holy things.

David was educated to the priesthood, first at the Celtic monastery of Henfynyw (Hen Vynyw), and then under Paulus the Scribe. He proved to be a very able scholar and other students said that they saw angels whispering in his ear, urging him on in his studies. He would have appeared to take a great interest in the aesthetic lives of the early Desert Fathers in the Egyptian wilderness and this seems to have formed his religious practices for the rest of his life He also undertook several long missionary journeys to other holy houses including Glastonbury before returning to Wales to found his own monastery. There is some dispute as to where this particular foundation was located. Some authorities say that it was at Glyn Rhosin whilst others say it was at an uncertain place named 'Menevia' (now thought to be site of the modern-day city of St. David's). Wherever it was, life there was very hard for David's disciples as he was a stern taskmaster. His Rule followed that of the most arduous aspects of the devotions of the Desert Fathers and he demanded total obedience from all those who followed him. In a time when many monasteries made their own wine and beer, David forbade his monks to drink anything other than water, earning him the nickname *Aquaticus* (Waterman); when working in the fields, they were to do so without oxen, yoking their own bodies to the plough; as an act of contrition and belief, they were to stand naked for hours on end in the freezing snow. Their diet was to consist of bread, herbs, salt and water – no meat whatsoever – to be consumed in utter silence. In fact, silence was more or less the order amongst them, since no man was to speak one to another except it was absolutely necessary. Personal possessions were absolutely forbidden. David's discipleship was not an easy one to follow. However, there is little doubt that he was a great an inspiring preacher, possessing an eloquence not usually heard amongst ministers of the day. It was his oratory at the Synod of Brevi (Llanddewi Brefi) that firmly established David as one of

the foremost Christian speakers of his day. Although supposed to be formal debates determining the policy and
dogma of the Church, Synods sometimes tended to be noisy
and unruly places with delegates shouting each other down
or to make themselves heard over the tumult and in fact
adding to it. At Brevi, large numbers of representatives and
their followers turned up and the din was overwhelming.
Bishops were forced to stand on piles of coats and other
clothing in order to make themselves heard and even at
that many of their words were ignored in the shouting. Each
bishop tried to make himself sound more important than
the others.

David had not intended to attend the Synod but after
much persuasion eventually agreed to do so. Ignoring the
great and mighty bishops on their heaps of coats and robes,
David made his way to the centre of the throng where he
laid a small piece of cloth upon the ground and stood upon
it. Instantly, the ground began to rise under his feet until it
formed a small hill, carrying David above the heads of the
delegates. In a small, low voice that hushed the surrounding riot, the saint spoke eloquently but firmly and, as he
did, a dove descended from the Heavens and settled on his
shoulder, remaining with him throughout his oratory. This
was taken to be a symbol of Divine approval for his words.

Although widely known and respected as a holy figure,
David nevertheless returned to Menevia to live the life of
a simple monk. It is said that he now made an arduous
pilgrimage to Jerusalem where he was consecrated as a
Bishop or Archbishop by the Patriarch John III, but this
story is now largely discounted. Nothing is known about
his death but it is known that he had a the earliest *Life of
David* that can be traced was written by Rhygyvarch, son
of Julien, who was bishop of St. David's in 1090. By this
time the town, dedicated to the saint, had become a thriving and relatively prosperous place, firmly on the Celtic
sea routes, which linked Ireland, Brittany, Cornwall and

Scotland with parts of Continental Europe and already en-
vious eyes, both spiritual and commercial, were being cast
in its direction from England. Rhygyvarch's motive for writing the *Life* was a political one. The diocese of Canterbury
was beginning to look towards Wales as part of its ecclesiastical territory and the Abbot wished to retain Welsh independence from the English. He sought to strengthen
both the cult and legend of David in order to give the saint
some sort of national identity. And it was a successful ploy.
Later *Lives*, extolling David's holiness were written and were
included in the lives of other saints – for example St. Paul
Aurelian and his cause appears to have been taken up by
Asser, King Alfred's confessor and bishop. The case for the
holy man and his distinctive Welshness was growing
steadily. Soon it would be brought to the attention of Rome.

The cult of David was approved by Pope Callistus II in
1120 and the reputed bones of the saint – then held at St.
David's – were classed as holy relics and it was declared
by Papal Decree that two pilgrimages to St. David's shrine
was worth one to Rome. The ruling firmly preserved Welsh
ecclesiastical independence from Canterbury and established St. David's as an important site on the pilgrim trail.
David was well on the way to becoming the national saint
of Wales. The influence of his cult began to spread all across
the Celtic world and missionaries from his foundations –
especially from those in Wales itself – set out for destinations such as Ireland and Cornwall to carry the message to
these parts. Dewi Sant was now widely regarded as the
national saint of Wales.

The relics of David were translated twice – first in 1131
and again in 1275, by Richard Carew, Bishop of St. David's
who rebuilt the Cathedral there largely from donations at
the shrine. Important pilgrims made their way to worship
at the site – these included several English kings, William I and Henry II on his way to and from Ireland. Their
presence showed the importance of the saint to English

religious thinking. The influence of David was now extending right across Wales and into the English countryside and many religious houses, including the foundation at Glastonbury, claimed him as their patron.

The imagery of David usually depicts him standing on a small hill, with a dove upon his shoulder, as he did at the Synod of Brevi. Yet, there is no real tradition connecting him with either leeks or daffodils, both of which are also Welsh symbols. According to Shakespeare, these are incredibly ancient traditions 'based upon an honourable request', yet no satisfactory is given for their origin and there seems to be nothing to associate them with David. The Feast Day of the saint is, nevertheless, established as 1st March, supposedly the day on which he died, although there are some suggestions that the date has a much older tradition. The name 'David' is often rendered in Welsh as 'Daffyd' hence the nickname 'Taffy' which is often given to Welshmen, especially those living abroad or in England.

Like Patrick before him, David's message was a stark and simple one – all Mankind must prepare for the Second Coming, which was imminent. Christ would return and would expect His disciples to have led an exemplary life, which included prayer and fasting. The flesh must be mortified in order that the spirit might be exalted. He is often represented as an austere and unbending individual and yet as Dewi Sant, he served as an exemplar of a pure faith, a light and an inspiration to many. And as St. David his simplicity has come to symbolize what is best and attractive about the Welsh nation.

Chapter 8

DYMPNA

Even by Celtic standards, the legend of St. Dympna of Gheel is a strange one and shows the early church in a somewhat different light to the works of the first holy men. Unlike many of these, St. Dympna did not found an influential monastery, nor was she associated with great missionary works. And yet, under her patronage much admirable and valuable work has been carried on. She is the patron saint of lunatics and the insane and much of their care is carried on in her name. It is even uncertain that St. Dympna existed and yet her legend was so powerful that it acquired a cult following in the 13th century. In essence the legend is as follows:

Dympna is said to have lived in the seventh century, the daughter of an Irish pagan king and a Christian mother, both unnamed. Exactly where in Ireland she was born is unknown but the times were said to be very turbulent in the area in which she lived. At a very early age, she decided that she too wished to become a Christian, but because of her father's views, she was baptized in secret. It is not known exactly who baptized her but she is said to have privately expressed the wish to enter Holy Orders. However, once again, she kept this wish a secret from her father.

As she approached puberty, her mother took ill with a wasting disease and died. Her mother had been extremely beautiful and it caused Dympna much suffering to see her lose her looks and fade away. Her father was distraught with grief and turned towards Dympna for comfort. At first the girl looked after him but then she began to suspect that her father was not wholly thinking of her as a daughter. She was extremely beautiful and looked very like her mother and the king was seeking a replacement for the wife that he'd lost. That replacement was to be his own daughter. In Celtic society, women held a position of some importance – they had more defined and greater rights than women elsewhere in the ancient world. Yet every woman still had to obey her king and this was an extremely sensitive situation. Horrified Dympna realized that she was in an impossible position. She was determined not to give into her father's incestuous demands and she was equally determined to maintain her Christian faith. She did the only thing that she could – she fled the court, aided by a courtier and his wife. They made their way to a nearby small Christian community led by a holy man named Gerebern. In fact, it may have been Gerebern or his father who had secretly baptized Dympna herself. The king, however, learned of her whereabouts and the tiny Christian community scattered. Dympna went with Gerebern, the unnamed courtier and his wife.

The party fled to Gheel in Flanders, near to the present-day city of Antwerp in Belgium. During a plague that swept through the region, the courtier and his wife died but Dympna and Gerebern were spared. Trying to put the awful events behind her, Dympna threw herself into good works particularly the care of the sick. She had a special affinity with those who were epileptic and insane. And she cared for them on a daily basis becoming, in effect, one of the first psychiatric nurses. By losing herself amongst the diseased and the mentally ill, Dympna hoped that she was free from her father's strange obsession. It was a vain hope.

Her father was still trying to find out where she was so that he could force his will upon her. He sent out emissaries and spies to all parts of Britain and the Continent and finally, through some clever detective work, he managed to find out where she was. Tradition says that he had issued his own distinctive coinage, struck with his own head on it, and it was through this that he traced Dympna to Gheel. Now that he knew where she was, he wasted no time in pursuit. Catching up with her, he issued a royal command that she marry him. Once again Dympna refused and she fled once more together with Gerebern to live as hermits in a heavily wooded area beyond Gheel. There they lived a simple life where Dympna, in common with many other Celtic saints, was protected by natural elements – rivers changed courses, forest animals hid her tracks to prevent pursuit. But the king, now driven almost insane with lust, tracked them both down once more.

For a third and last time, he commanded that his daughter should marry him and once again she refused. She revealed to him then that she was a Christian and could not obey his commands The king then accused Gerebern of sullying his daughter and had him killed. In grief and pain, he himself then slew Dympna, cutting off her head and declaring that he if could not have her, than no one should, not even God. For this terrible blasphemy, he was afterwards struck down. Dympna died with her faith and honour still intact.

According to legend, a series of miracles took place after these dreadful murders. Many local people in the Gheel region, appalled and horrified by what had happened discovered that the bodies of both Dympna and Gerebern had been removed from the murder site and placed in two marble tombs which held splendid coffins and which were said to have been constructed by angels at God's behest. Whist the tombs themselves disappeared, the coffins were removed and kept at Gheel.

Over the years, the couple became revered and minor pilgrimages to the town began to occur. Sometime during the 11th or 12th centuries, the coffins were plundered by grave-robbers who tried to removed both sets of remains but succeeded only with those of Gerebern which were carried as far as Sousbeck in the Rhineland where they are still retained. Around Gheel the veneration towards the single coffin of Dympna increased as did the pilgrimages to it. The area became a shrine, generating much income for the town. A hospital, caring for epileptics and the mentally ill was built and was dedicated to her. Even today, Gheel has an exemplary record for the care in this area. Pioneering treatments and the development of care of mentally disturbed patients in their homes have all been carried out there.

During the 13th century the cult of Dympna seems to have become very widespread. Pilgrimages to her shrine increased dramatically and the legend of her death was circulating all through France and even into England and Ireland. She was declared a martyr and a saint and her Feast Day was declared as 15th May. In fact, pilgrimages are still made to her shrine on that date and her relics are still kept in a silver reliquary within a church which bears her name. Besides the church and mental hospital at Gheel, altars dedicated to Dympna are to be found at Hasselt, St. Quentin and Herck-la-Ville in Belgium. There are a number of holy wells in both Belgium and France, which are dedicated to her, the waters of which are believed to cure epilepsy.

This is the legend of Dympna for which there is not a shred of historical evidence. In fact, it could be that there was really no such person and that the entire tale is a work of fiction. Certainly, there are tangible relics which are attributed to the saint, but there is really nothing – no real evidence – to link them with a person called Dympna.

There is a suspicion that they might be from a slightly later period than the seventh century and may be connected with someone else, maybe even some other saint whose name has been lost. But there is no evidence one way or the other. No *Life of Dympna* exists and there are none of the widespread monastic foundations, which were said to have been established by the saint. Nor does she appear to any great extent in any of the medieval calendars that detailed established saints (the hospital at Gheel was erected long after her martyrdom). The foundation for her (admittedly quite strong) cult is solely based on the legend of the virgin martyr.

Undoubtedly, psychiatrists and mental workers will be able to analyse the legend and see various traits within it – the incestuous father pursuing his daughter has obvious Freudian overtones – whilst folklorists will draw parallels with the Irish legend of Dermaid and Grainne who fled from the aging Fionn McCumhaill and with numerous other legends across the Celtic world. Students of literature will no doubt see the first stirrings of the doomed medieval romance.

Perhaps the story of Dympna *is* an attempt to Christianise old pagan myths, such as Dermaid and Grainne, and to give them a more moral standpoint. If this is true, then the attempt seems to have succeeded for the legend was certainly a 13th century potboiler. Feminists may see in the saint the personification of a strong and defiant woman who refused to surrender her principles in the face of authority. And perhaps *that* is her real strength and the real source of the legend.

Following the Synod of Whitby in AD 664, women had to find a new role for themselves within the Church. Previously women had been allowed to hold a position of some authority within the Celtic Church – they were allowed to preach, to hold high office and even (as in St. Bridget's case) become abbesses and church leaders. Under the dogma of the Roman Church they appeared to have been relegated to a more subservient role. What they needed was a role model – a woman who could stand up to the authority of a now largely male dominated Church. The template for this may not have lain within Christianity at all but within the old pagan martyrdom legends. And so one of these became adapted into a Christian tradition – a widespread Christian story without any evidence of the Christian world. And its origins lay in the confusion and aspirations of Celtic Christian women. During the 12th and 13th centuries, as the last vestiges of the Celtic Church tradition began to finally fade away, this motif once again found a renewed expression and the cult of Dympna began to grow and develop once more. This, of course, is only a theory but it is a plausible one.

There is, however, one curious thing concerning the saint. Although there are no monastic foundations attributed to the saint in either England or the Continent, there *is* at least one in Ireland, though it is presently in ruins. Just north of Monaghan town and south of Armagh, lie the remaining fallen stones of St. Dympna's Abbey. The date of its founding or the name of its founder (as it was certainly not the saint herself) are unknown. And it was here that another relic – the saint's crozier – was supposed to have been held. And this brings in another curious tradition. The crozier was said to be an extremely ornate one – studded with jewels – and the country people of the area if accused of a crime, such as stealing, were required to come and swear their innocence upon it. If they swore falsely, then their mouths were supernaturally and permanently twisted out of shape, marking them as a liar for the rest of their lives. In effect, the relic became a sort of medieval lie detector. No trace remains of this marvelous staff; and it is rumoured to have been carried off or destroyed during the conflicts that marred the region in the late 1500/early 1600s. Some scholars suggest that the naming of the foundation may relate to another St. Dympna but are unable to refer to another holy woman of the same name. Incidentally, a similar crozier, the bachall (staff) of an unnamed saint, with exactly the same powers was to be found at the ancient church of Ardclinis on the east Antrim coast. It too was lost, but has since been recovered and is now in the National Museum in Dublin.

Today, St. Dympna and her cult remain and intriguing enigma – a mystery which may never be solved.

Chapter 9

HILDA

If there is a patron of arts and scholarship amongst the Celtic saints, then St. Hilda of Whitby must surely be one of the foremost contenders. More importantly, she is counted as a great reformer in the church and her convent of Whitby was the site of the famous Synod, which united both the Celtic and Roman churches. Her importance to the Church has been recognized by the celebrated scholar and historian, the Venerable Bede Hilda was born in Northumbria in AD 614, and like many other Celtic saints, came from a wealthy background. In fact, she was a princess of the Deiron dynasty and a grandniece of King Edwin of Northumbria and was also related to the East Anglian Royal Family. Her parents seem to have spent part of their lives in exile in the British enclave of Elmet (in what is now North Yorkshire) but Hilda seems to have spent much of her early life in East Anglia before moving to rejoin her parents in Northumbria. And it was in Northumbria that she was baptized by the monk Paulinus (a disciple of St. Aidan on the island of Iona) who had arrived there in the year 629 following the conversion to Christianity of King Edwin and Queen Ethelbruga. Their conversion was a controversial one since many of the surrounding pagan kings wished to destroy the Christian religion and to stamp out any of its adherents. Shortly after becoming a Christian, Edwin was defeated in battle by a confederation of these kings and the religion found itself under threat.

In 663, Oswald, Edwin's nephew, Oswald (later patron of St. Aidan) decided to confront the pagan confederation in battle. The armies met at Hexham near Hadrian's Wall and it is said that on the night before the battle, Oswald had a vision of the Irish saint Columcille who assured him of victory on the following day. The prophecy came true, Oswald was victorious and he sent to Iona for a missionary to come and convert his people. That missionary turned out to be St. Aidan.

With Christianity establishing itself in the North of England, Hilda's religious future seemed secure. She traveled to the court of her cousin, King Anna of East Anglia to be tutored in the ways of the Church. The East Anglian church was an offshoot of the Irish one and followed a purely Celtic doctrine in which Hilda was instructed. Whilst in East Anglia, Hilda decided to join the convent at Chelles in France, where her sister Hereswitha was a member of the community.

It is said that St. Aidan himself visited her in France, having recognized her abilities as a leader, and persuaded her to return to Northumbria. After much prayer and thought she agreed and came back to found a small abbey on a plot of land on the northern bank of the River Weir, the exact location of which has been forgotten. She only stayed there a brief while before moving to Hartlepool where she succeeded Heiu as abbess. The Rule of living which she adopted there took its source from both Irish and Gaulish monasteries and may have followed the example of St. Colum.

In 657, she founded or re-founded the abbey at Whitby, which became a dual monastic site catering for both monks and nuns. It would seem that there might have been a former abbey on the site which had fallen into neglect or else had been destroyed and abandoned during the brutal wars and conflicts that ravaged that part of Britain. The new abbess was given the task of restoring the abbey to its former status. Under Hilda's leadership, it was to become famous as

a centre for learning and study and for training and conse-
crating at least five bishops of the early church, including
St. John of Beverley. 'Even kings and princes asked for and
accepted her advice,' observed Bede. And she encouraged
the creative arts as well, including oratory and poetry. One
of her protégés was the poet Caedmon who had worked as
a servant at Whitby but whom Hilda encouraged to become
a monk. Hilda supported his 'vernacular poetry about the
Christian doctrine'. She also encouraged widespread study
of Scripture; she was well read herself, not only in the Bible
but also in the works of the Early Fathers of the Church
and could offer opinion and interpretation on them 'as well
as any man'. The reputation of her foundation and of Hilda
herself spread across England and into the Roman and
Celtic worlds in general.

Because of its reputation for scholarship and learning,
Whitby was chosen as the location of the Great Synod of
AD 664. This was summoned by King Osby of
Northumberland to settle a dispute concerning the date of
Easter. This Feast had been held on different dates by the
Roman and Celtic churches but it became the focus of various other disagreements between them – such as the con-
secration of bishops and the organization of diocese. As
the Synod progressed, however, even more differences
came to the fore – the admission of women to the priesthood; the importance of Confession; the method of celebration of the Mass, all crying out to be addressed. These had
all been largely minor differences between the two
churches but now they flared into the open with a particular vehemence. Most of the important churchmen of the
day were there – Colman of Lindisfarne, Chad of Lichfield,
Wilfrid of York and Agilbert of the West Saxons, each of
them ready to offer a weighty opinion on these matters as
befitted their august status within the Church. Rapidly it
descended into two camps – Roman and Celtic – and it
soon became clear that this would become one of the most

important such gatherings of the century. The Synod convened at the end of 663 with Hilda playing host. With her immense respect, learning and experience, she was called on for opinion and she supported the Celtic position, particularly the Irish and Scots delegates but 'she was gracious to all'.

The Synod was a contentious and acrimonious one with clear differences emerging between the two factions. Even when it had ended, a number of Celtic clerics refused to accept its decisions. The most notable was, of course, St. Colman of Lindisfarne who actually vacated his abbotship in protest. Indeed, a number of other Synods had to be held centuries later in Ireland – for example the first Synod of Cashel – to resolve still outstanding issues. Hilda, however, stated that she would fully accept whatever decisions the Synod of Whitby achieved.

It was King Osby himself who finally settled the disputes in favour of the Roman Church but the Synod had been heated and acrimonious and many personal hatreds and jealousies had been exposed. One of these was Hilda's own dislike for Wilfrid; Bishop of York whom she thought had manipulated the Synod to increase his own ecclesiastical power. When Theodore of Canterbury divided the Northumbrian see in favour of St. Bosa and St. John of Beverley, Hilda supported him against Wilfrid. The matter was subsequently rescinded on the direct orders of the Pope but in the year 703, the Synod of Austerfield (West Yorkshire), presided over by Archbishop Bertwald deprived him of his see once more and although eventually once again restored in 705, the experience left him an ill and broken man. By this time, of course, Hilda was long dead and yet, it was said, that not even death could stem her influence.

Although Osby's ruling had effectively made the Roman Church supreme and therefore the position of women much less than it had been before under the Celtic regime, Hilda still continued to enjoy a position of some status. She was left pretty much to develop her foundation at Whitby as she saw fit. Her counsel was still much sought after, not only by temporal rulers but also now by churchmen as well. She developed a wide reputation for knowledge and learning and also for giving sage advice. It might well have been tempting in these turbulent ecclesiastical times – and it appears that Hilda was a consummate political animal – to ally herself with the burgeoning anti-Roman feeling in certain quarters of the Church. However, having given her word that she would accept the Synod of Whitby's conclusions, Hilda was as good as her promise, even though it is doubtful whether things had turned out as she would have wished. She still continued to patronize the arts and Whitby remained a centre for culture and scholarship. In an ecclesiastical world which was coming to be increasingly dominated by men, she was a woman of remarkable vision and status.

Hilda survived the Synod of Whitby by about seven years but was extremely ill. The date of her death is uncertain with some accounts stating around AD 671 and others asserting 680 The Venerable Bede states that a nun called Begu, heard a bell ringing in the middle of the night and rose to witness Hilda's soul ascending into Heaven. The other nuns were gathered and they prayed until morning when monks arrived with news of Hilda's death Her Feast Day was proclaimed as 17th November, supposedly the day of her death (although several other dates are mentioned and may have been kept elsewhere) and her remains were interred within the abbey of Whitby.

Although the last years of her life had been marked by chronic illness, her spirit was not diminished. She abided by the decision of the Synod of Whitby and whilst her own religious life followed the pattern of Irish and Frankish worship, she gradually introduced Roman practices and ethos into the daily routine of her foundation. Her successors Elfleda (daughter of the Northumbrian

king Oswin) and Enflada (daughter of King Edwin) com-
pleted the processes that she had begun. By the mid-700s,
Whitby was an example of one of the well-functioning
Roman foundation in all of England. Its fame under its
new abbesses is recorded in the first *Life* of Pope Gregory the Great, written about twenty-five or so years after Hilda's death.

Around the year 800, Whitby was attacked by Viking
raiders. It was to suffer repeatedly at the hands of the
Norsemen throughout succeeding years. So much so, that
the abbey itself was completely burned to the ground and
many of its treasures carried off as booty. Around this time,
Hilda's remains seem to have disappeared. No one is completely sure what happened to them – they may have been
destroyed by the Vikings ort they may have been removed
by monks prior to the attacks and reburied in some secret
location in order to protect them. There is a rumour that they
may have been taken to Glastonbury for a while, under the
protection of King Edmund who died in 946; but there is
also a strand of legend, which says that they were removed
to Gloucester. There are other legends still that they were
taken to some unspecified location to be reinterred.

The Abbey of Whitby was re-established, not as a dual
monastery in the Irish style (as it had been in Hilda's
time) but simply as a holy house for monks, in the 11th
century. Nevertheless, Hilda appears to have left a thriving cult behind her. A number of ancient churches were
also established in her name – the names of fifteen of
them in England still survive. There were also eleven
such sites in Yorkshire and two in Durham. The earliest
identification of a cult of Hilda appears in the ancient
Calendar of St. Willibrord, which was written sometime
in the 8th century.

Throughout her life, Hilda seems to have been a remarkable woman and one with considerable foresight. From
earliest times, she came to recognize the importance of

education and art, which would characterize the Church throughout the medieval period. And she was politically skilled enough to make her views and wishes have influence but in a subtle way, not by the bluster and disagreement which had dominated the Synod of Whitby. As one of the foremost women of what are now known as the Dark Ages in England, her influence was incalculable.

Chapter 10

KEVIN

Each year, the large, early-Irish monastic site of Glendalough in Co. Wicklow draws large numbers of visitors from all over the world. Yet, though impressive as the surviving buildings of what was once a monastic city are, they are associated with a saint who exemplified the ideal of the early hermits and who is often upheld as the epitome of humility and sacrifice. Even so, little is really known about the life of St. Kevin – the Latin and Irish *Lives* upon which scholars rely date from at least 400 years after his death. Furthermore, they were written for a specific purpose – to further the claims of Glendalough, then an important monastic site, and of the saint himself. They are a mixture of legends and probable half-truths that tell little about the man and his works. The actual figure of Kevin himself is badly obscured by holy legend and blatant propaganda.

However, some facts do seem to be known. Although the date of his birth is unclear (variants give it as somewhere between AD 492 and 498), it is known that his birthname was Coemghen, which in ancient Irish means 'of gentle birth'. He was born in Ireland, most probably into a reasonably wealthy and well-educated family somewhere around the late sixth century. As with everything else about his life, the circumstances of his birth are shrouded in legend.

Some sources say that he was born into the Royal House

of Leinster and that twelve angels bearing golden lamps attended his entry into the world; others state that he was the son of a chieftain and also mention that angels appeared as he was being born.

Nonetheless, tradition suggests that he was born to a noble Leinster family (sometimes given as Dal Mesincorb), which had been ousted from the kingship, and that from childhood he was educated by monks. That same tradition also asserts that from a very early age, he was fascinated by the lives of the Desert Fathers and by the hardships and privations which they endured. Once again, legend states that at his baptism the priest, Cronan (who gave him the name Kevin as commanded by an angel) prophesied that the child would be a great force for God in the world and that kings and priests would come to Christ through him.

Kevin is said to have spent his early years at the Fort of the White Fountain. No actual location is given for this site and the names of it vary but it is thought to have belonged to Kevin's father and was a stronghold. Whilst there, Kevin was allegedly visited by St. Petroc from Cornwall who had been told in a dream to travel to Ireland behold a new light in the Christian world. It is said that Petroc became Kevin's teacher for a time. The boy showed a special aptitude for poetry and music, especially for the harp. When he was roughly seven years of age, the boy was sent to the monastery of Kilmanagh, near Tallaght, Co. Dublin. Amongst the monks who taught there were St. Enda, St. Eoghan and St. Loughan, all influential figures in their own right within the Celtic church. Once again, he demonstrated an intense interest in the lives of the Desert Fathers and was exceptionally holy and devout in his ways.

At the age of twelve, Kevin is supposed to have left the monastery and went to visit three hermits living at Usneach (Usny Hill, Co. Westmeath). Some variations of this legend give these holy men as three saints who had a profound influence on Kevin. – Columbia, Comgall and

Cannich. His fascination with the hermit life was now evident and it's said that he lived with these recluses for several years. One story concerning him comes from this time – he was told to bring embers from a fire in order to light candles for the Mass and was tardy in doing so. Angrily, he was told to bring them on the corner of his cloak and the boy obeyed. However, there were no burn marks whatsoever on the material and the hermits realized that this was no ordinary child but that the Holy Spirit dwelt within him. Returning to Tallaght, he was ordained as a priest and told that he could remain there as an instructor to young novices. Nevertheless, apparently guided by God, he left Tallaght, late in the year 544, and set out for the monastery of Clonmacnoise, There, the abbot St. Ciaran was said to be one of the holiest men in Ireland.

Keviv arrived at the foundation in the Spring of AD 545 to find that Ciaran had died three days earlier. Some other legends state that he arrived just as Clara was dying and that the holy man gave him a bell as a token of great saintliness.

Turning away from Clonmacnoise, Kevin headed for the Wicklow Hills. Here, in a remote and extremely lonely glen known as 'the Glen of Two Loughs' – Glendalough – he began the ascetic life of a hermit, trying as best he could to emulate the privations of the Desert Fathers. He would only wear the skins of wild animals and would only eat what he could gather from the surrounding trees and plants.

It is thought that he settled near the upper lough in the valley where 'St. Kevin's Bed' is to be found today. He is believed to have slept on a stone and used another stone for a pillow. It's also said that it was his custom to stand in the freezing waters of the lough, reciting the Psalms and keeping vigil. Afterwards he would retired to a narrow cave in order to pray – the idea of retreating into caves in order to talk with God was a very common one in the Celtic church, used by both St. Patrick and St. Ninian. The route from the lough up to this cave was extremely overgrown and dangerous but legend states that an angel moved before him, clearing the way and establishing a path for him to pass. Today the cave is accessible by boat but still requires a steep climb over difficult terrain.

All traces of Kevin's original monastic settlement, Teampull na Skellig (the rock chapel – which was originally a Bronze Age fortification) have been lost amid the ruins of various other monastic establishments belonging to a later date.

For years, Kevin lived in the valley in complete isolation. There are many stories and legends about how his whereabouts were discovered. One of the most prevalent concerns a local chieftain called Dimma who had a custom of grazing his cows in an area close to where Kevin had his hermitage. One of them was supposed to wander down to where the saint was residing and would lick his robes as recognition of his holiness. Each morning thereafter, the animal would give much more milk and of a richer quality than any of the other cattle and Dimma was at a loss to explain it. He instructed one of his herdsmen to follow the creature and to find out the pasture where she fed. The man did so and thus Kevin's hermitage was discovered. The saint pleaded with Dimma not to reveal where he was, but the chieftain soon made the location widely known.

Kevin's reputation for saintliness spread all across Ireland and soon he began to attract a number of followers. Disciples began to arrive in the lonely glen in large numbers and after seven years of isolation the saint felt that he had to move to a more habitable spot to accommodate them. It is said that he also found the nearness of people distracting and unbearable and that for a time he moved to a remote part of Argyll in order to be alone in prayer and meditation.

He was – allegedly – called back to Glendalough to deal with a monster which had supposedly appeared in the Upper Lough. In folklore, this creature was a great serpent with dripping fangs, which was harassing those of Kevin's followers who still dwelt by the lough shore. Kevin is said to have defeated the monster and banished it – making him the saint who cast the last serpent out of Ireland instead of St. Patrick. The story of the serpents being cast out as recorded by the monk Jocelyn was an amalgamation of a number of old wonder tales as is attributed to a number of saints.

Throughout his ministry, Kevin remained chaste – although a number of women tried to distract him from his holy contemplation. In order to prove his holiness and firmness of purpose, it is said that the saint took two young virgins to his bed each night leaving them untouched in the morning. On hearing of this, St. Brendan, tried the same test but was kept up all night by 'the promptings of the flesh' and was forced to roll in a bed of nettles to take away carnal urges. One woman, Kathleen, became so enamoured of St. Kevin that he took her to a lofty height above the upper lough and threw her in, drowning her. (Such tales as these are in line with the stories of the Desert Fathers, who were frequently tormented by demons in the form of carnal lusts and desires and by their saintliness over came them. The most famous of all the anchorites so tempted was St. Anthony of Egypt.)

Glendalough was now becoming a place of great pilgrimage and the fame of Kevin was spreading. Other monastic foundations began to appear and the saint withdrew more and more into the wild. It was said that he was offered the abbotship of the main monastic foundation but refused, preferring the life of an ascetic hermit than that of a formal abbot. Other sources recount how he accepted the abbotship but really took no part in the life of the monastery, apart from establishing a Rule under which the monks could live.

Like many of the other early saints, Kevin established the harmony with the natural world, which was very much a part of the Celtic response to God. Stories about him accentuate both his love for and power over animals and plants. The most famous story reflecting this concerns a blackbird. It was Kevin's custom to stand in the freezing waters of the Upper Lough, his arms outstretched in an imitation of Christ, whilst praying and meditating. One day the bird settled in his open palm, built herself a nest there and laid an egg. Patient and gentle towards all living creatures Kevin waited, refusing to move until the tiny bird had hatched, grown and flown away. Another legend tells how a boy in Kevin's care asked for an apple in the middle of Winter. The saint turned to a nearby apple tree, which was then bare, and blessed it whereupon it immediately bore fruit and the boy's request was granted.

St. Kevin died around AD 618, reputedly at an advanced age anywhere between one-hundred-and-twenty and one-hundred-and-sixty. Yet, before his death, he is said to have returned to the site of his original hermitage, a wild and lonely place but one where he felt most at home. His monks carried whatever meager food he need to him but gradually he became weaker and eventually he slipped away and left the world. Although he had founded several other monasteries, the one at Glendalough was the most important and its reputation spread throughout Ireland. A veritable monastic city grew up there. It extended around the Lower Lough, becoming one of the major pilgrimage centers in Ireland. It also became a centre for study – the most celebrated student there being St. Laurence O'Toole (1128–1180) who later went on to become Archbishop of Dublin. Kevin was declared a saint with a Feast Day on the 3rd June.

Although he was not a famous missionary in the style of some other saints, having spent most of his life at Glendalough, Kevin's influence on the Celtic church was considerable. Arguably, more than any other saint, he exemplified the founding ethos of the Desert Fathers and by his humble and pious life, showed the true path of simple Faith.

Chapter 11

MAELRUAIN

By the beginning of the 8th century, Celtic monasticism was in a mess. Although the Synod of Whitby (AD 664) had sought to bring some sort of harmony and uniformity to the Celtic and Roman Churches, in truth it had achieved very little. Many religious foundations were still under the control of abbots with bishops still relegated to a secondary position. A number of these abbots were eccentric people to say the least and their Rules for monastic life reflected this. Monasteries ranged from fairly liberal dual foundations which accommodated both men and women to places such as Glendalough where mainly men came to study and where an extremely strict. The Celtic Church as a whole, however, had become extremely lax and even corrupt. There was no unity or cohesion anywhere. Moreover, Celtic monasteries had to compete for disciples with the more regimented and co-ordinated Orders, which had arrived from the Continent – the Augustinians, the Benedictines and latterly the Dominicans. Faced with such opposition, the Celtic monastic system was near to collapse. What was needed was a rigorous, disciplined Order within the Celtic church.

In the mid-to-late 7th century, an attempt was made in Ireland to establish such an Order and thus bring a measure of cohesion to the fractured Church. Its founder was St. Maelriain (Mael-Ruain) of Tallaght. In many ways, Maelruiine is a strange figure – virtually nothing is known about his life and no miraculous legends have attached themselves to his life and yet his writings, which survived him, were probably amongst the most influential within the Celtic church of the time. The Order which he founded was the *Ceili De* – 'the Friends of God', later Anglicised as Culdee – and it remains the only known ordered Celtic monastic brotherhood.

It is not known where Maelruain was born, nor is anything known about his early life as a monk, though it is surmised that he may have come from a monastery in Munster and was related to the Ui Mall clan who had connections in the Glen of Imaal in Co. Wicklow It is not known, however, where he studied or who his early teachers might have been. But it would appear that her was influenced by the mysticism, which characterized the Celtic Church coupled with the disciplined outlook of the early Desert Fathers. Although his character also remains a mystery, he emerges as a stern and severe figure, austere and inflexible regarding matters of Faith.

He appears to have been a person of some influence. For example, in the year 775 he was able to procure lands in Tallaght (Co. Wicklow) from Cellach mac Dunchada, King of Leinster. Here, he built a monastery, installing himself as abbot. This was the first holy house in which he established the Rule of the Ceili-De. This was a strictly ascetic way of life, which concentrated on three principal elements – prayer, study and work. It skillfully combined those elements of the spiritual tradition with a rigid, hard-edged, demanding discipleship. A saying ascribed to Maelruain underlined his philosophy and his view of the holy life. It ran thus:

'Do not eat until you hunger; do not sleep until you are ready for it; speak to no one without just cause'

Worship was centred around repetitions of the Palters and genuflections and primacy was given to community prayer.

Stress was placed upon the notion of 'enclosure' and the Culdees were to take no interest in the outside world. If, for example, a visitor were to call at one of their foundations, the monks were not permitted to ask if he had come far or where he was from since that might imply an interest in worldly affairs. Likewise, pilgrimage to other places such as shrine were expressly forbidden. This was an understandable response, as the notion of pilgrimages had become largely a matter of abuse within the Celtic world with monks getting drunk and conducting themselves disgracefully when away from their monasteries.

This notion of enclosure did not, however, discourage other Culdee foundations from being established. The monastery at Tallaght was the first of three Irish houses along the River Shannon – the other two being Finglass and Terryglass, all of them following the same strict Rule. During his lifetime, Maelruain is credited with producing a number of writing, which were influential in the reforming impulse of his movement. These included *The Teaching of Mael-Ruain* and *The Rule of the Ceili-De* and were outlines for monastic life and worship.

Later, the Culdees themselves were to produce a number of important works detailing their life and outlook: the *Martyology of Tallaght*, being produced one year after Maelruain's death; and the *Stowe Missal.*

The Rule of Maelruain also revealed the saint's prejudices. For instance, he seems to have been implacably opposed to women having any involvement whatsoever within the Church, even to the receiving of the Sacrament. During the 8th and 9th centuries, as the Roman Church began to develop its dogma, a fierce debate raged as to whether women should receive the Host during their 'unclean time' (menstrual period) which was viewed as a punishment from God for Original Sin. The Celtic Church had always been fairly lax in these matters, even allowing women to act as priest and to dispense the Sacrament. Maeleuain was implacably opposed to inclusion of women in all but the most peripheral forms of worship, referring to them as 'men's guardian devils'. Consequently, the Culdees were an exclusively male Order.

The saint also seems to have been strongly opposed to the Roman Church. Whilst espousing Roman discipline and striving for a kind of Roman uniformity, he was nonetheless at pains to preserve the mystical and contemplative elements of the Celtic faith. Confession was not the sole preserve of the priest but absolution could be achieved through a 'soul-friend' (a confidant which surprisingly included women); his monastery's devotional life placed particular emphasis upon the person of the Virgin and of St. Michael; the Sacrament of the Mass was held in a slightly different way; alcohol (a common feature in both Roman and Celtic foundations) was expressly forbidden and the Celtic Sabbath (Saturday) was rigorously observed in preference to the Roman one (Sunday). This Celtic distinctiveness would later lead to the Culdees being branded as 'dangerous nationalists' by the incoming Roman Orders and there is little doubt that a separate nationalist identity played a part in their view of the world.

Life amongst the Culdees was harsh. There was particular emphasis on self-examination and self-punishment, with flagellation recommended and monks were required to observe vigils standing in freezing water with arms outstretched in an imitation of Christ on the Cross. There was also a strong emphasis on work, both intellectual and physical. Monks worked tirelessly at jobs such as gardening or sewing clothes. They also both wrote and studied – as said Maelruain:

The Kingdom of Heaven is granted to him who directs study, who studies and who supports the student'

Because of the enclosed nature of their Order and the

emphasis on self-reflection, the Culdees produced marvelous poetic works mostly based in Nature, which best reflected their relationship with God. Possibly the most famous of the Culdees writers was St. Aengus (Oengus) who lived at the end of the 8th century and who collaborated with Maelruain on the *Martyrology of Tallaght* as well as being author of the *Felire (Festology) of the Saints*, a poetical work which now forms part of the later *Leabhar Brac* (the Speckled Book). He dwelt more or less as a hermit at Dysart-Enos, a remote oratory near Maryyborough (now Port Laoise, Co. Laoise). Later, Culdees were to commemorate his life in the *Martyrology of Oengius*.

Despite the severity of the Rule, monks flocked to Tallaght to study under Maelruain and the Culdee movement grew. Other oratories began to appear – one of the most significant at Youghal, Co. Cork and gradually their influence began to spread out across Ireland.

Maelruain died on 7th July of the year 792 (which became his Feast Day) and left behind a reforming movement which, although still relatively haphazard, was gradually forming an effective counterpoint to the Roman Church and which was upholding Celtic traditions. Although they had founded certain monasteries of their own, many of the Culdees attached themselves to other religious houses and worked their reform within them.

It was the arrival of the Normans in Ireland in the mid-12th century, which effectively dealt the deathblow to the Culdees as a widespread movement. The fledgling Order had been established too late in the day and had been forced to compete with other more established foundations, which had come in from England, all of whom regarded the Culdees as 'heretics' The dogmatic regimentation of say the Augustinians and Dominicans suited the Norman barons who were anxious to increase their power by forging links between Church and State. Furthermore, the nationalistic ethos and zeal of the Culdee

Order was regarded with some alarm by the Norman military machine. They joined with the Roman Orders in denouncing the Culdees and in driving them out. In 1183 for example, the Norman noble John de Courcey expelled an entire foundation of them from the precincts of Down Cathedral in Ulster and installed the Benedictines with whom he had close links.

The Culdees fled westwards, many of them either seeking out lonely parts of Ireland in which to set up new foundations or else leaving the country altogether. Many of them went into the Western Isles or into the West of Scotland and it is known that they had a foundation at Dunkeld. It's also suspected that some of them dwelt in the Highlands where they lived as hermits and that they had an influence on the Celtic identity of the North of Scotland. Others traveled as far south as York, which is the only place in England where there has been a Culdee settlement. Some of them did, however, remain in Ireland as the sites of their foundations (for example at Kiladees in Co. Fermanagh – the name means Church of the Culdees) attest. A few of them continued to exist unmolested and some of their abbots achieved a fair degree of prominence in local communities. In Armagh, there was a Culdee house near the Cathedral until the mid-1500s and its abbot; Rauri MacGillamurragh served on the city's Board of Public Works. This explains the two thoroughfares, Culdee Street and Culdee Terrace in the city precincts.

Even a thousand years after his death, Maelruain continued to cause controversy. Pilgrimages were made to his shrine in Tallaght and this was actually encouraged by the Irish church.

The shrine itself was said to have been built for MacRaith O'Donoghue, King of Cashel and for Donagh, son of Brian Boru by a monk, Donchad O'Taccain of Clonmacnoise, and was a splendid affair. However, things began to change in the early 1800s, when an old Dublin piper with the splendid name of Burley O'Toole was laid to rest in the churchyard close by.

O'Toole had left instructions that each year there was to be a procession and ceilidh (party) for musicians at his grave and this was carried out. The name of the saint had also been wrongly given as 'Moll Rooney' and had become confused with a summer festival in this name which involved dancing at a pole garlanded with flowers. The gatherings soon got out of hand, and there was so much drunkenness and faction fighting that the police were frequently called to the church property. Many of those taking part in 'bawdiness and licentiousness' were pilgrims at the shrine. Church officials said that the Feast Day had 'become a more excuse for drunkenness and debauchery'. In July 1873, the local priest, Father Purcell, closed the shrine and pilgrimages ceased. The site is now an Anglican church, which still bears the saint's name. The Shrine is now in the National Museum in Dublin.

Because of their strict enclosure and the fact that some of their penitential rituals were held in secret, the Culdees became associated with witchcraft and sorcery – although this was probably no more than propaganda diseminated by other Orders. The Culdees were reputedly the guardians of several mystical 'bachalls' (the staffs of holy men), which had been given into their care. In 1820, during the building of the currently-existing church, cavities were discovered containing human skulls, a chalice of glass and a medal showing a human figure holding a staff aloft. No explanation has ever been given for these items! Maelruain and the sect that he founded remain as much an enigma today as they did in former times.

Chapter 12

MALACHY

By the late 11th and early 12th centuries, the Celtic Church, now largely Romanised but still retaining some elements of its former identity had become more settled. Taking its example from the Roman Church, it had drawn closer to the kings of Ireland who ensured both protection and patronage for it. Nevertheless, it was steadily losing ground to Roman organization and it looked as though any Celtic distinctiveness, which it still retained, might be subsumed in a wholly Roman church. The great Synod of Rath Breasill (1111) now insisted that canon law was to be the basis of local and overall government within Ireland; that all Irish marriages were to be stable, legal contracts (and there were to me no Celtic 'trial marriages' for a year and a day, nor marrying between close relatives as was sometimes the Celtic practice); that clerics were not allowed to marry; that the practices of Confession and Confirmation were to be renewed throughout the country and that Roman chants were to be introduced in the liturgy. All of these had previously been neglected due to disputes within the Church and repeated Viking invasions. Many Celtic monastic houses too – such as the great abbey founded by St. Comgall at Bangor – had been destroyed during these raids and had not been restored; Celtic libraries had vanished and monks had been scattered. Someone would have to pull the shattered Church together and impose some sort of discipline upon it, whilst at the same time maintaining its distinctiveness if it was to survive in any form. That someone was St. Malachy.

Malachy O'Morgain (Maol Maedoc) was born in Ireland around 1094 probably somewhere near Armagh. His father is given as Mughron Ua Morgain, a noted teacher and Irish noble with the title of 'Chief Lector of Armagh and of the West of Europe' whilst his mother's family owned the lands on which stood the abandoned abbey of Bangor. His older brother Giollacroist would become Bishop of Clogher and his family was said to be one of the most educated in Ireland. Given such a background, how could Malachy not turn to the Church and to Church Law?

Malachy's father died in Limerick when he was eight years old but by then the boy had set his sights on the religious life. He studied under the best teachers of his day in Ireland and was eventually ordained around 1119. Much of his study had been on Church Law and he was deeply interested in bringing some sort of order to a faith that had apparently grown lax. He traveled to the abbey of Lismore, Co. Waterford, where he further studied law under the direction of St. Malchus, archbishop of Cashel and a former monk at Winchester.

In 1123, he received from his uncle, the lands and ruined abbey of Bangor in Co. Down, which had long been deserted. Malachy accepted the ruin but refused the tithes and rents from the land. Instead, he concentrated on reestablishing the foundation and with the help of ten monks from Armagh built a small wooden church there. In 1134, he was consecrated as Bishop of Connor (and Down) but he still continued to live in Bangor. In his new diocese, he was faced with a shortage of worthy priests and a great laxity within the local Church. The Sacraments had been neglected and local pagan customs were still being observed; church tithes were not being paid. Malachy worked to reform the diocese but his efforts were frustrated by a local chieftain, who eventually drove both him and his monks out. Accompanied by 120 monks he made his way to Munster where King Cormac of Desmond granted him lands for another monastery – possibly Ballinaskelligs in Co. Kerry.

It was a time when reform was in the air, not only within the Celtic Church as it stirred to reassert itself but also within the Roman faith which itself had become indolent and lax. Fifty years earlier, one of the most important of the early medieval Popes, Gregory VII (1073–1085), had been elected to the Holy See and had been determined to bring Christianity into line. Through the decisions of the Lenten Synods of 1074 and 1075, he had attempted to deal with corruption within the clergy and in his pronouncement *Dictatus Papae* (March 1075) he outlined and strengthened the position of the Pope, together with the authority of the Church. As a student of Church Law, Malachy read and was impressed by the Pope's reforming work and zeal and was determined to emulate it in Ireland. His vision was that of a strong Irish church with the regimentation and discipline of Rome but with a distinctive Celtic ethos. To do this, however, he had to be in a position of influence within the Irish Church and that influence lay not in Ballinaskelligs but in Armagh.

The monastery at Ballinaskeeligs, however, became the centre for one of Malachy's experiments – the establishment of the Austin Canons in Ireland. These were a branch of the Augustinian Order, which had established and cohesive rules for religious life. They pursued the Celtic values of poverty, celibacy and obedience but did so without withdrawing from the world. There was also a great emphasis on study, just as there had been in the early Celtic monasteries. Their blend of pastoral care and educational outlook provided a desired regularization of life for monks. Gradually, they began to live in Cathedral towns and to conduct their business amongst ordinary people.

In 1129, Cellach, the Archbishop of Armagh died and

Malachy saw his chance to spread the Gregorian Reform all across Ireland. By this time he had returned to Bangor, as it was now safe for him to do so, and was able to put himself forward for the vacant post. Indeed, he was Cellach's named successor. Nevertheless, his accession was not an easy one. The Archbishopric of Armagh had become almost a family business and one of Cellach's relatives, Muirchertach, also laid claim to the title. He was supported by a number of local chieftains and most of Cellach's family. Gilbert of Limerick, the Papal Legate, who could have determined the outcome, sat on the fence and refused to give a decision as to who should succeed Cellach. Part of the opposition to Malachy sprang from his insistence on the Gregorian Reform and his links with the Augustinians who were perceived largely as a Roman Order and not a Celtic one. The situation could have led to outright warfare but for three years, Malachy skillfully avoided this. In the end, Gilbert overcame his reluctance and named Malachy as Archbishop of Armagh. An armed peace existed between the two camps until Muirchertach's death in 1134. His successor and kinsman Niall, although he accepted the Legate's decision, held onto the *Beculam Iesu* (the Staff of Jesus, the crozier and symbol of authority of the Archbishops of Armagh), together with the venerable *Book of Armagh*, thus assuring himself of some recognition in the North even though the south of Ireland was solidly behind Malachy. With the Irish Church now badly riven between Roman and Celtic elements, Malachy felt that he had to resign in 1137 – in favour of Gilla, Abbot of Derry, who was more acceptable to both factions.

Malachy returned to Down, where he established a monastic site at Downpatrick, which was, once again, to become highly significant at bridging the gap between Roman and Celtic perspectives. He was still determined to press ahead with reform and he decided to travel to Rome itself, via Scotland and York, to receive confirmation from the Pope. He set out possibly around 1138, taking with him a number of trusted friends. The papal reign of Gregory VII had ended in exile and confusion and he had been succeeded by a number of relatively weak Popes more concerned with secular politics and internal power struggles than Church reform. The Pontiff whom Malachy hoped to meet was Innocent II (1130–1143), who was more concerned with the machinations of the anti-pope Anacletus II who had been elected by the Reform lobby in the Vatican. Innocent, it has to be said, was hardly sympathetic to Malachy's views but he was seeking support to restore the developing schism in the Roman church Malachy thought that he might be able to use this to his advantage.

On his way to Rome, Malachy stopped off at the Cisterian abbey of Clairveaux in France. Its abbot and founder St. Bernard was deeply interested in Celtic mysticism and encouraged a form of mystical prayer amongst his monks. Bernard and Malachy became great friends. With Bernard's good wishes, Malachy traveled on to Rome. His meeting with Innocent was highly unsatisfactory. The Pope had little interest either in Irish reform or in the Irish Church in general and appeared aloof and distant to the Irish representatives. Ireland was still a physically isolated area and was consequently only of marginal interest to a Continental Pontiff such as Innocent. Malachy asked if he might join with Bernard's monastery at Clairveaux, but the Pope refused and instructed his return to Ireland to sort out the bishops and clergy there. At the meeting Malachy also applied for a *pallia* or Bishop's cloak for both the Archbishoprics of Connor and Armagh (this would have strengthened his position in Ireland) but once more the Pope refused.

Greatly dispirited Malachy returned to Ireland via Clairveaux. Bernard was great distressed to hear of the failure of the mission and agreed to accept five on Malachy's companions who might be trained as Cistercians. In 1142, some of them would return to Ireland together with French monks to found the great abbey at Mellifont in Co. Louth. This foundation was to become famous for it magnificent buildings and learned monks. Those who came from it were skilled in both farming and building methods. Even in its early years, Mellifont was one of the largest and most impressive abbeys in Ireland and was frequented by nobles and kings including, it is said, the High Kings of Ireland. Other Irish Cistercian foundations were established in Newry (Co. Down); Bective (Co. Meath) and Boyle (Co. Roscommon).

Near the end of 1143, word reached Ireland that Innocent II had died. Malachy decided that it was time to go to Rome again as the next Pope might be more sympathetic to his cause. He hastily convened the Synod of Inishpatrick, near Dublin, which gave him the necessary authority to travel to the Holy See. The Synod also instructed him to reapply for the *pallia* once more. Two of Innocents successors, Celestine II (1143–44) and Lucius II (1144–45) enjoyed extremely short reigns and so it Pope Eugenius III (1145–1153) whom Malachy set out to see. This time he was reasonably confident of success – Eugenius was a Cistercian and a friend of Bernard of Clairveaux. However, the Pontiff spent only part of his time in Rome and so the visit had to be timed correctly.

In 1148, Malachy and his monks reached Clairveaux once more where Bernard was delighted to see them. Malachy was both weary and ill and was glad of the rest. Whilst at the monastery, Malachy succumbed to a fever and died in the arms of his friend Bernard of Clairvieaux, who would afterwards become his biographer.

Malachy was cannonised in 1190 by Pope Clement III. Although he died on November 2nd, his Feast is held on November 3rd so as not to conflict with All Souls Day. His Feast is kept by the Cistercians, the Canons Regular of the Lateran and throughout Ireland.

A number of miracles were attributed to him during his lifetime. Whilst returning home from Rome, he is said to have cured Prince Henry, grandson of St. Margaret of Scotland. He is said to have told the boy: 'Be of good courage, you will not die this time'. Perhaps the most famous supernatural story attached to his name is that concerning a series of prophesies detailing the line of Popes from 1143 to the end of the world. This was said to have been revealed to him in a vision in 1139. The 110th prophecy is *De Labore Solis – 'from the Toil of the Sun'* – Pope John Paul II was born on 8th May 1920 during a solar eclipse. To date, only two of these prophesies remain unfulfilled. It is, however, doubtful if these had anything to do with the saint but are from a much later period.

The cult of Malachy, fostered by Bernard of Clairveaux, became highly influential in the Middle Ages. Its growth, and that of the monasteries that he founded, still bear tribute to a remarkable and reforming saint.

Chapter 13

MUNGO/KENTIGERN

The person of St. Kentigern is slightly difficult to establish, partly because he is also known by another name – St. Mungo – and because many of the sources about him tend to be more folkloric than historical. All of these sources date from the 11th and 12th centuries but contain elements which are considerably older and which may not even refer to Kentigern at all.

Records state that Kentigern died in the early 7th century (possibly around AD 612) and that much of his work was carried out in the areas of Strathclyde and Cumbria however, few actual facts are given about his life. It is also stated that he is British and that his father was a noble prince, probably called Urien (maybe even the celebrated Northern king, Urien Rheged, although the dates are suspect), although the name Loth (Lot – perhaps Lot Luwddoc, King of Goddodin) has also been given. Folklore states that his mother was named Tannoch who was to marry another chieftain but who decided to forego that honour in order to become a Christian and keep herself chaste. According to the legend, she was hunted down and violated by the chieftain whom she was to marry, becoming pregnant as a result. Outraged, her father tried to kill her by pushing her, in a wagon, over a 700-foot (over 330 metres) drop called Dunpelder on the southern side of Traprain Law near Haddington in Lothian. The girl, however, called to the Virgin Mary and, although the wagon was shattered into pieces, she miraculously emerged unscathed. Still her father was determined that she should died because of her shame and set her adrift in a coracle from Aberlady Bay, drifting towards the Isle of May. Tides and winds carried it into the Forth of Culross where it was brought ashore by monks from the foundation of St. Serf. It was in a settlement on the edge of this foundation that Tannoch is supposed to have given birth to a boy in the year 518. The child was taken to the aged St. Serf himself and the old man was said to have been 'filled with spiritual laughter and in his heart with joy' at the very sight of the infant.

The above story of Kentigern's birth is in all probability no more than a legend and can be attributed to a number of other saints. However, there are strong indications that he was of illegitimate birth and there it is actually recorded that he was 'educated in the Scriptures' by 'Serf of Culross'. He does not appear to have been a popular student, however and some legends hint that he may have suffered from a physical deformity that made him the butt of jokes amongst the other novices who gathered around Serf. His piety, however, was not in question and a number of minor miracles are attributed to him around this time. One of these concerned a tame bird, which belonged to St. Serf himself. When the holy man was away from the foundation some of the more boisterous novices captured the bird and literally tore its head off. Shocked by what they had done, they made a pact to blame Kentigern for the misdeed. The boy took the battered body in his hands, made the sign of the Cross over it and prayed fervently. Instantly the bird was restored to life, was made whole again and flew to meet Serf on his return. Although Serf had baptized the child as Kentigern, he also called him by the name Mungo, meaning 'my dear friend' and this became a kind of pet name that stuck with the saint throughout his life.

Whether it was due to a physical deformity which set him apart from other novices or whether it was the attention paid to him by his teacher, Kentigern became more and more unpopular with his peers. At last the resentment became unbearable and he secretly left Culross. Soon after he encountered St. Fergus of Carnock. Fergus was ailing when the two met and soon had fallen grievously sick. The young Kentigern ministered to the ancient man and when Fergus finally died was said to yoke a cart to two untamed bulls, which he then drove eastwards. At last, he came to a ruined and overgrown cemetery that had nonetheless been blessed by St. Ninian over one hundred years before. It was at this stream, the Burn of Molendinas, that Kentigern buried Fergus and set about rebuilding and re-establishing a church, which had fallen into neglect and disrepair. Gradually, a community grew up around the rebuilt church, which became known as 'Eglais ghu' or 'Glesghu' meaning 'dear church' or 'dear family', the forerunner of the modern-day city of Glasgow. From this settlement missionaries went out across Scotland but the times were greatly unsettled and the Christian message met with much opposition from warring local kings. Eventually, it was decided by several local rulers that there was need for a bishop who would hopefully bring stability to the region. Kentigern (or Mungo as he was now known) was chosen to fill that role and around AD 545, he was consecrated as Bishop of Strathclyde by an Irish bishop.

Despite his Installation as bishop, the situation in the area deteriorated even further and Kentigern struggled to hold his mission together.

Around this time, fantastic stories concerning the saint's holy powers seem to have evolved. A prevalent one concerned his prophesy to a queen who had given her husband's ring to her lover. On recovering the ring from the lover, the king threw it out of the window towards the sea and told his unfaithful wife that if she didn't find it in three days, he would kill her for her infidelity. Though she looked for it, she couldn't find where it had fallen.

Distraught, she consulted Kentigern. The holy man told her not to worry as the ring would be back in her possession before three days were past. One of his monks had caught a salmon, which had the ring in its belly. So widespread was the tale that it forms the origin of the symbols of the ring and the fish that appear on the coat of arms of Glasgow – a city which still claims Kentigern (Mungo) as its own. However, this is probably no more than a holy wonder tale, without foundation, designed to enhance the saint's reputation.

Although he was now a bishop, Kentigern lived the simple life of a hermit. His lifestyle, and that of his disciples, mirrored that of the Desert Fathers in Egypt and was austere and demanding. Kentigern foreswore any luxury or comfort, dressed in a shirt of uncomfortable horsehair and goatskin with a white alb and cowl on top. His staff was of plain wood without any ornament and he always wore a stole as a symbol of his humility. He chose to live in a small hut that contained only a rock on which he slept and he spent his mornings reciting the Psalms whilst standing in the freezing waters of a river, which flowed by his door. It was a life of extreme penance and hardship but it was a spiritual example to all those around him.

As the political system around him grew steadily worse, Kentigern decided that he should move further south and began to make his way to Wales. During his journey there, he is credited with founding several churches as he passed – such as on the site of present-day Mungrisdale. The senior Christian figure in Wales was St. David whose ministry was already seven years old when Kentigern arrived. David welcomed him as a fellow Christian and helped him to found a community at Llanelwy, now known as St. Asaph's. The site of the new community was determined by a pure white boar which both the holy men had been following that stopped on a hillside and began to paw the ground. Kentigern immediately declared that this was a divine oracle and this was where the church should be built.

According to tradition, the tiny church that Kentigern raised blossomed into one of the most important monasteries in North Wales with over 1,000 monks in its cloisters. This is highly unlikely, as is the assertion that he was consecrated as the first bishop of St. Asaph's. These stories were later additions and there is no liturgical evidence of a strong cult of either Kentigern or Mungo in Wales.

According to tradition, it was Kentigern who foresaw the death of St. David over which he shed tears of grief. He saw David's soul progressing to Heaven on a road of light and later when word was sent to Menevia, it was found that the vision was completely correct. David was already dead. News of his visions and omens traveled around Celtic Britain and the great Northern king Ryderech Hael, sent word to Kentigern asking him to come to him as an oracle. In return the saint could found a monastery in the North of England. Kentigern was tempted but one night he experienced a dream in which an angel voice told him to go back to Glasgow, 'to thy Church'. Leaving Asaph as his successor in Wales, Kentigern set out for Scotland. He did not, however, return to Glasgow but settled at Hoddam in Dumfries and Galloway where he conducted a new mission. After several years there, he received a formal call to return to Glasgow and was reinstated as its bishop, even though he'd been gone for over thirty years. From here, he sent out an evangelic mission into Aberdeenshire and is said to have personally led Christian expeditions into the Western Isles, to Orkney, Iceland and Norway. There is no evidence that Kentigern went there – in his later years he seems to have been extremely infirm – but it is possible that some of his followers did go to these places.

Tradition says that both Kentigern and Columcille (another important and influential Celtic saint) and that the two of them exchanged bachalls (crosiers). It is said that Columcille (Columba) and his monks were descending a certain hill whilst Kentigern and his followers were ascending. The site of their meeting is said to be marked by a well, known as St. Mungo's Well, which is reputed to have many healing properties. There may be some truth in this tale since the two saints were contemporaries and were operating in a roughly similar region. However, there is no formal record of their meeting in any ancient text.

As he grew older and even more infirm, Kentigern's body became more and more wasted, so that it 'grieved his followers to see him'. He passed away in a bath of warm water, a measure which he had requested 'in order to heat his blood' in chilly weather and his soul was said to have been lifted into Paradise immediately. Some biographers give his age as 185 but it is more probable that he was roughly in his eighty-fifth year. His burial site is now part of Glasgow Cathedral. Legions of angels were said to be seen over his church in order to bear his spirit aloft.

There are several ancient Scottish sites dedicated to St. Kentigern (Mungo) and nine in England, mainly in Cumbria and there are also a number of wells in the Western Isles that bear his name as Mungo though it is doubtful that the saint himself was ever there. Ancient ecclesiastical calendars give his Feast Day as 13th January.

Kentigern may have lived his life as a simple monk but his influence in Scotland and the North of England was formidable. Aside from the holy houses, which he founded, he is said to have maintained the 'Irish liturgy' in many of the Northern monasteries. Even after his death, his monks followed Celtic Irish traditions of prayer and psalms that continued for hundreds of years. For example, the Bollandists, a group of Catholic academics have published a series of liturgical praises dedicated to St. Kentigern and dating from the 13th century that are couched in an 'Irish' framework. And yet, he remains an enigmatic figure, as obscure and mythical as the times in which he lived.

Chapter 14

PATRICK

Although Ireland's patron saint, St. Patrick's origins are uncertain. Certainly a native Celt, he is nevertheless thought to belong to Roman Britain. Even though both his grandfather, Potitius, and his fathe, Calpurnius, were both officers of the early Church, there is little evidence that Patrick showed much inclination towards the religious life.

By his own admission he was lazy and indolent and neglectful of his Christian upbringing. His family was a wealthy one, allegedly owning a small estate at Bennavieum Taberniae, thought to have been on the British west coast and it was here that Patrick was said to have been born around AD 390. The coast was frequently under attack, however, from Irish raiders in search of cattle and slaves. During one such raid – whether by Irish pirates or by the forces of the Irish High King, Niall of the Nine Hostages – the sixteen-year old Patrick was captured. Taken back to Ireland, he was one of those sold into slavery to Milchu (Miliuc), a local chieftain who held lands around Sliabh Mis (Slemish Mountain) in Co. Antrim. On the slopes of the volcanic mountain, legend says that he tended the swine of his pagan master for just over six years. Life was hard and often during the rain, storm and freezing snow, he thought of his home and of the Christian faith – which sustained him across this miserable time. At some stage during his captivity he was believed to have met with

Caranoc, a monk of Cadida Casa, identified as St. Ninian's foundation at Whithorn, whom the *Book of Ballymote* (written around 1390) identifies as one of the first Christians in Ireland. The holy man seems to have made a great impact on the young slave and legend states that Caranoc baptized him as a Christian deacon sometime around AD 411 or 412. Patrick was also inspired to escape his captivity and he managed to walk over 200 miles to the esturary of the River Vartry near Wicklow where at a seaport, he joined the crew of a ship bound for Gaul (France). After traveling for almost thirty days through the Gualish countryside he was eventually taken in, weak with hunger, by the Christian community at Lerins, on the island of St. Honorat, where he later served as a deacon. He was still ministering here when he received a call to return to Ireland.

The call came from the great teaching foundation at Auxerre in France, where Patrick is also said to have studied. It was said that it was actually here that Patrick had been ordained a deacon by Amator, a predecessor of the celebrated St. Germanus of Auxerre, who had seen a great promise in the former slave. Irish missionaries had been writing to the Pope, Celestine I, advising him that the church in Ireland needed structure and organization if it was to survive and if it was to counteract heresies, which were already breeding there. The Pope wrote directly to Germanus and asked him to send a bishop to Ireland as soon as possible.

Although Patrick had received dreams and visions, which suggested that he might go to Ireland, he was not the one that Germanus sent. Instead, Germanus consecrated Palladius, a Gaulish Celt, as Bishop with instructions to set sail for Ireland. Whether Palladius ever reached the shores of Ireland is unclear. It is thought that he may have stopped off in Britain where he succumbed to a virulent plague, which was raging there; other opinions state that he may have preached briefly in Ireland before dying from disease. Patrick's dreams, however, increased and he was now convinced that he should be chosen to go to Ireland. As indeed he was for shortly after, at Avrolled, he was consecrated Bishop and was dispatched as Palladius's successor. With him went two other priests – Auxillius and Secondinius – to serve him in his ministry.

It is not clear as to when or where he arrived in Ireland but tradition states that it was around the year 432 and that he landed somewhere near Strangford Lough in the north of the country – although other traditions have him landing in Wexford. There is no doubt that his years of Irish captivity had prepared him for the job – he probably spoke the language and knew Irish society and customs well, which appealed to the local chieftains. Ireland was at this time a turbulent country in which localized warlords constantly grappled for territory and status – some of them may have seen Patrick as an enemy; others may have viewed him and the God he represented as an ally. Patrick himself was probably politically astute enough to use both sides to his advantage in the spread of the Christian message. He set about organizing and co-ordinating the various disparate mission stations, which were scattered throughout the land and his knowledge of local geography may have aided him in this. His message was stark and simple – the End of the World is coming when Christ will return and all Mankind should prepare for it. His dogma owned more to Rome than it did to the Celtic tradition and yet it was adaptable enough to embrace and retain many elements of the latter forming a Church that was largely Celtic in nature.

One legend concerning him tells of how Patrick returned to Slemish, the site of his former captivity. On hearing of his return, his former master Milchu committed suicide but his son accepted the new religion and granted the saint land on which to found a mission. On the spectacular site of the now ruined medieval Skerries Church, Patrick received his mission and his crozier (a symbol of his authority in Ireland) directly from an angel and from there he set out. The footprint left by the angel is to be seen in the Rock of Skeery to this day. Legend further states that his first preaching mission was located at Saul in Co. Down – near present day Downpatrick The name Saul means 'barn' and it was supposed to have been a kind of shed given to him by a chieftain, Dichu. From this humble site the Christian message spread out across the Irish countryside. However, a case is also to be made for the spread of the religion from Ard Magh (Armagh) where Patrick is also thought to have maintained a missionary school on land granted to him by Daire, one of the Ulster kings.

The majority of Ireland, however, remained pagan and the High Kings of Ireland still looked towards the druids of the old pre-Christian religions for guidance. On Easter Day, 25th March 433, the clash between King Laoghaire and Patrick took place when the Saint lit a paschal or Easter fire close to the Hill of Tara, seat of the Irish High Kings. This was also the pagan Spring Festival during which all fires across Ireland were extinguished and then relit from one kindled by the High King himself on the Hill of Tara. In lighting his fire before Laoghaire, Patrick not only challenged the spirituality of the King's druids but also the authority of the monarch himself. As the fire roared up on the Hill of Slane, in full view of Laoghaire and his warriors, the druids warned that if this fire were not extinguished, it would burn in Ireland forever.

There followed a contest between Patrick and the druid magicians from which the Saint emerged triumphant. Even so King Laoghaire refused to be convinced and died a pagan but his brother Conal Gulban was baptized by the Saint and acted as his protector. The story of the Paschal Fire, however, has no real basis in history and may have been a later monkish addition to draw parallels between

Patrick and the druids and the Biblical tale of Elijah and the priests of Baal.

Many miracles were attributed to Patrick as the Christian religion took hold – the most famous being that he drove snakes out of Ireland. Again this is a monkish invention (both Roman and Greek geographers concur that there were never any snakes in ancient Ireland), written about the mid-12th century by Jocylen of Furness – an English monk who had never been to Ireland. Another legend states that he taught the lesson of the Trinity using the shamrock as its symbol, this once more is probably ecclesiastical invention written many centuries later to demonstrate the holiness of the man.

Most of Patrick's missionary work appears to have been in the North of Ireland although wells and other sites are credited to him everywhere from Derry to Kerry. There is no doubt that he accomplished many great feats, the most politically important being the rise of Ard Macha, which was later to become a principal stronghold of the Ui Niall (O'Neill) dynasty of the Irish High Kings and where his shrine was said to have been preserved. It is thought to have been Secondinius, his helper, who became the first bishop there whilst Auxillius, his other companion, was buried at Saul. Patrick himself is said to have died aged 112 – although the date of his death is sometime given as AD 493 (other sources cite 461) – receiving the Body of Christ from the hands of the holy Bishop Tassach, whom he himself had baptized. There is no real record as to where he was buried although there seems to be some dispute over his body shortly after his death and several of his bones seem to have been taken back to the stronghold of Armagh where they became an object of adoration and pilgrimage. The various *comarbs* or Bishops of the Cult of Patrick, kept the memory of the saint alive through stories of alleged miracles and immense sanctity.

It was the Ui Niall who turned Patrick into the patron said of Ireland. Under their kingship in the ninth and tenth centuries, the cult of Patrick in Armagh flourished. There were other contenders for the overall sainthood – Brigid and Columcille – but these were too 'Celtic' and too flawed to become a national saint and to unite the Roman and Celtic ethos (Columcille had started a bloody war, Brigid was a woman). It was Patrick, with his Roman credentials but who had also been active in the Celtic world, which appealed to both Churches.

By adopting Patrick as their saint, the politically astute Ui Niall kings brought together the Celtic tradition and the now largely Romanised Christian church behind them, enhancing their rule. At one time, Armagh actually challenged Iona as the centre of Celtic Christianity in the Western World. Repeated raids on Patrick's shrine by Viking bands greatly increased its status as a spiritual site and that of its Saint as a Christian icon. Although his feast day was taken from the Calendar of Metrologies as the 17th March (reputedly the date of his death), there were many disputes and for centuries, the monks of Chester celebrated it on 24th March whilst at Glastonbury it was kept on 24th August. There is also a translation citing it as the 10th June. In Ireland, however, it was kept as the 17th March placing it between the feast-days of those other two fully Celtic saints – Brigid and Columcille (Columba). Patrick's famous crozier – the 'Bachall Iosa' or Staff of Jesus – which he had received from the angel on the Skerries Rock, was publicly burnt in 1538 as an 'example of Popery' during the reign of the Protestant English king Henry VIII.

The simple message that Patrick brought with him has now been overlaid with myth and dogma so that it is difficult to see the original saint. He was not the first Christian to preach in Ireland but he may have been the first to organize and consolidate the early Christian church within the country. And there is no doubt also, as with many other national saints, that he was later used for political ends. This has made scholars begin to question the existence of

Patrick – for example it's even suggested today that Patrick may not have been a single man at all but a number who bore the title *Patricus* meaning 'father' or 'noble'. Whatever the truth of it, there is no doubt that Patrick remains one of the best known and much-loved saints all across Ireland and far beyond.

Chapter 15

PETROC

If Cornwall were to have a national saint, then that honour would probably fall on St. Petroc, arguably the most influential of all Cornish saints. Although St. Michael is usually taken to be the symbol of the Cornish people (as in St. Michael's Mount) and was venerated throughout the Celtic world, he remains an angel, a supernatural being, whereas Petroc was an actual man about whom we know a little.

Petroc lived in the 6th century and he came to Cornwall from South Wales. Tradition hints that he was of the Welsh Royal Household of Gwent and that his uncle was St. Cadoc. Whilst this is questionable, he probably did come from a Christian background and had adopted a Christian lifestyle from an early age. It is also possible that he came from a reasonably wealthy background and was fairly well educated.

It is thought that before coming to Cornwall, he studied extensively in Ireland, remaining there was more than twenty years. Following this, he crossed the sea, landing at Haylemouth and founded a church beside the Camel Estuary in Cornwall in a religious settlement – which he called Petrocstow but today has become Padstow. About 30 years later, he founded another monastery at Little Petherick which he called Nanceveton and which included another church and a large mill.

Following the foundation of the community at Padstow, it appears that Petroc went off on certain religious 'pilgrimages'.

Folklore speaks of a journey to Rome and to Jerusalem. And there is also a rather bizarre and fanciful story about him living as a hermit on an island in the middle of the Indian Ocean. It seems that whilst he was traveling, he fell asleep on board a boat and, allegedly on waking, saw a large silver bowl floating towards his vessel over the waves. Climbing over the boat's side, Petroc lowered himself into the silver bowl, which now seems to have taken on gigantic proportions and the receptacle floated away, taking him to a remote island. There he lived for seven years living solely on fish, which he ate but were miraculously returned each day to the ocean. At the end of seven years, the bowl returned and carried him back to the land to which his vessel had been sailing. There was his staff and robe (which he had left behind) being guarded by a wolf. When he returned to Cornwall, this tame creature accompanied him and though it looked fierce, it hurt none. Indeed, in common, with many other Celtic saints, Petroc is supposed to have had a calming influence on many wild animals – wolves, bears, wild pigs and later, as we shall see, dragons, The tale of the fabulous journey is, of course, an invention but it has been used to account for Petroc's frequent absences from his church and for his probable 'wanderings' outside Cornwall.

One of the kings of Cornwall was Teudar, a fierce, cruel and totally irreligious leader. And yet this same warlord was terrified of Petroc. Perhaps he feared the holy man's alleged supernatural powers because Teudar was also deeply superstitious. The saint demanded that the tyrant give him a parcel of land, which he put together with another land-gift that he'd obtained from Constantine, a more sympathetic local ruler. Using these gifts, he built a hermitage on Bodmin Moor, which he called Bosvenegh – 'the place of the monks' to which he retired for a time. The story concerning Constantine is a common one in the annals of religious Celtic folklore. One day whilst out on pilgrimage, Petroc beheld a fawn which was being chased by some particularly savage hounds and, in pity for the creature, threw his cloak around it. The hunting band, led by Constantine, arrived to find only the holy hermit standing there and were so impressed by Petroc's sanctity and purity that they were immediately converted to Christianity. At the request of the saint, the monarch handed over a large portion of land so that churches could be built and the new religion might be spread throughout the land. All this is, of course, highly unlikely (such tales are frequently used to explain why many pagan monarchs converted to Christianity) but there seems little doubt that Petroc was an eloquent orator and converted many, commoner and monarch alike, by the power of his words.

Living alone in his hermitage, Petroc became something of an oracle and a number of local kings are said to have approached him to learn their eventual fate for it is said that he answered every one honestly and all his predictions came to pass. However, he may have been no more than an astute reader of the political times and may have told each king what suited him. Nevertheless, he used his undoubted reputation as a force for good and for the furtherance of the Christian message. Many monks made pilgrimage to sit at his feet and learn from him. His influence spread out from Bodmin through Cornwall and into present-day Devon and Somerset as well. Indeed, monks seem to have carried his message and to have established foundations dedicated to him back in his native Wales.

Sensing that death was close and doubtless foreseeing his own end, Petroc set out on another pilgrimage to visit each of the communities that he'd founded in turn, to wish them well and offer advice for their continuance. Whilst near Little Petherick (known as Petroc Minor) he was suddenly taken ill and was forced to seek shelter in the house of a man named Rovel and his family. Though he was well tended, he did not recover and died in Rovel's hut in June 564. The site is still marked by a farm that bears the name of Treravel. His body was removed and was interred at Padstow but was later translated to Bodmin where he had built his hermitage. During the 11th century, the site where his relics were kept became a place of great pilgrimage and around them; a thriving cult dedicated to St. Petroc grew up. He was now one of the foremost Cornish saints.

In 1177, these relics were stolen by a Breton priest named Martin who is described in ecclesiastical texts as 'a malcontent Bodmin canon'. They were taken to an abbey at St. Meen in Brittany where, once again, they became something of an object of veneration. Bartholomew, Bishop of Exeter, investigated the theft and brought the matter to the attention of King Henry II who was actually overlord of the Breton Churches. Henry's influence was instrumental in returning most of the relics to Bodmin Priory, although certain bones were lodged in Bohemia, on the insistence that the saint had founded a monastery there as well.

The future archbishop of Rouen and then Justicar of England, Walter of Coutances, described the ornate reliquary in which the Bodmin relics resided. It was, he said, a fine ivory casket, carved in Sicilian-Islamic workmanship with a light inlay of gold. The bachall or staff of the holy man, together with a small hand-bell with which the saint called Mass, however were lost some time before the reign of Henry I and have never been found. It is said that the lost staff will confer upon whoever finds it, the power to 'still wild animals and the beasts of the field'. There are many other stories of further items associated with the saint, which have been lost to history. There are stories, for example, of a robe and a ring which still lie in the sea of the Cornish coast and which may protect England from invasion 'by barbarians'.

During the Reformation, the casket and its bones were hidden and were themselves lost for a time Petroc does not seem to have been a popular saint amongst English Protestants and his cult was probably persecuted. The relics were eventually found during the 19th century, hidden in the roof of Bodmin Church and have remained within its precincts since 1957. It now belongs to Bodmin Council and his counted to be one of the finest medieval reliquaries in existence in England today.

Mention of Petroc's cult and of his feast day (4th June) appear in a number of early West Country religious calendars as well as in the Canterbury books dating from the 11th century when the saint's cult appears to have been at its height. References to him appear in the Bosworth Psalter and the Missal of Robert of Jumieges. A record of his Feast Day is to be found in the Book of Hours of Pope Gregory XIII and in a 15th-century Italian Psalter. The saint was venerated in York, Ely and Bury where churches were dedicated to him and his Feast Day in June was observed. Both Exeter and Glastonbury both claimed relics but whether these were bona fide is open to question. As with certain other saints, there was some dispute as to his actual Feast Day with some churches claiming the 1st October (his first translation) and others 14th September (when his relics were returned from Brittany) as the actual celebrations. However, most authorities agree on 4th June.

Many depictions of St. Petroc show him standing beside a dragon and the saint has certainly strong folkloric connections with these fabulous beasts. For example, he is credited with removing a painful splinter from the eye of a great serpent and of taming the beast, which had previous been incredibly ferocious. Alternatively, he is credited with driving out the last Cornish dragon, a terrible monster, which had been terrorising Padstow. It is said that the saint either laid three reeds across its back (which turned into iron bands after much repeated prayer) or else bound it with a leather girdle with which he led it to the sea off Land's End, setting it free to swim away. Incidentally, exactly the same story is told of another Celtic saint, Murrough O'Heaney of Banagher in the North of Ireland. The Cornish version of the tale comes from a *Life of Petroc* written by the monks of Bodmin long after the saint's death and one tradition may well have borrowed from the other. Petroc is also supposed to have driven out a nest of dragons which had made their home on Bodmin Moor and he accomplished this through the power of his staff and through intense prayer. As he knelt to pray, says the legend, he was surrounded by the dragons' fiery breath and yet remained unconsumed because of his purity and holiness. The motif of the dragon or serpent is, of course, a strong one in early religious legend (as in the legend of St. George of England), symbolizing evil and darkness and one over which many of the Christian saints were supposed to achieve victory. The present-day 'obby-'oss' celebrations, which take place in Padstow on 1st May, are supposed to pay homage to St. George; but they may well have their true origins in the older legends concerning St. Petroc.

An ancient 'pilgrim's way' known as the 'Saint's Way' or the 'Forth an Syn' footpath, still in existence today, is also said to have its origins with the saint. The route runs from Padstow to Fowey and begins at the south door of Padstow parish church, which is believed to be the exact and actual site of Petroc's original monastic foundation. This is said to be part of the route, which Petroc took when he set off on his various pilgrimages in order to found his churches. It was said in early times that to follow this path would grant the devotee absolution from sin for a year and a day. There is no doubt from the ancient texts that Padstow was the centre of the saint's cult and that pilgrimages in his name continued there up almost until the late 16th century. And his influence also still lies far beyond the borders of Cornwall, as there are sites, churches, pilgrimage trails and wells still dedicated to him in Brittany, Wales and even in some parts of England. Even today, the name of St. Petroc continues to live on.

Chapter 16

PIRAN

St. Piran is probably the only holy man who can challenge St. Petroc as the patron saint of Cornwall. The Cornish national flag is known as 'St. Piran's Cross' and consists of a white cross on a black background and is taken as a representation of either silver or tin against the earth as well as the purity of the Christian faith in a world of darkness. Little, however, is known about the saint's life and times.

It is thought that Piran was born in either Ireland or Wales somewhere about the end of the 5th century. Nothing is known of his family or background except, like many of the Celtic saints, that it may have been a reasonably wealthy one owning estates along the coastline of the country. One of the earliest stories concerning him – and much of the records which we have about him, are simply a collection of folktales rather than genuine historical records – concerns a raid on his home by heathen raiders. Sometimes the identity of these raiders is given as 'wild Irishmen'. During the raid, the young Piran was strapped to a great millstone and carried to a towering cliff with the object of dumping him into the sea below and so drowning him. The heavy stone was pushed over the cliffedge but miraculously although it hit the ocean below with a mighty splash, the heavy stone didn't sink. Instead, under the astonished eyes of the raiders, it floated away with the saint still sitting on it. This was, it is reported, Piran's first miracle and a sign that, although very young, he was exceptionally holy and was protected by God.

The stone floated on across the sea until it reached the Cornish shore, landing at Perranporth on 5th March, which was to become the saint's Feast Day. It could be that the legend of the millstone might have its origins in the custom of some Irish missionary priests carrying consecrated stones with them when they arrived in a new land. These stones, blessed by a bishop and incised with the Christian Cross were very small, possibly no more than five or six inches across and were completely round like millstones, unlike the Saxon rectangular symbols.

For days the holy man lived amongst the sand dunes of the bay in which he had been washed up. He lived, according to legend, on whatever the sea gave him – there are stories of seals approaching him with freshly caught fish in their mouths – and he preached to whoever came near. It is said that in these sand-hills, he received a message from God, delivered by an angel, which said that he was to preach to the Cornish that lived round about and that he should minister as far away as Wales. Although deeming himself unworthy of such a mission, the saint accepted it and set about preparing for the holy life.

Piran built a small wooden chapel with an oratory near to where he had come ashore and lived there, with only a little food. He fist of all lived the life of a holy hermit but later on began to draw followers to him, to whom he preached. Perranporth may have resulted from a settlement of followers who stayed close to the saint's oratory to hear his words. This church and settlement appears to have grown into a small but influential monastic foundation of which Piran would have been the abbot. It was, in all probability one of the earliest such foundations on the Cornish coast and would have no doubt followed the tenets of the Celtic church. There is also a suggestion that Piran may have worked in metal – he is the patron saint of tinsmiths and his name was sometimes invoked to ensure that a metalwork job was done properly and without incident. The site of Piran's church was on sands, which gradually shifted and covered it up so for a while it was lost.

Nevertheless, legends of a 'Lost Church' (erroneously attributed to Saint Cairan of Saighair' (an Irish monk who had founded several monasteries in Ireland including Sierkieran, reputedly around 401 AD and a hermitage in Cape Clear, South West Cork) persisted along the Cornish coast. The remnants of Piran's settlement were rediscovered in the 16th century and again in 1830 when the sands shifted yet again. At this time, a full excavation was made and the ruins of the holy place were completely uncovered. This would make the church one of the oldest (if not **the** oldest) site of Christian worship in Britain. The ruins cannot be seen today as in 1980 they were reburied under unsightly concrete (they had been continuously vandalized) in order to preserve them. If nothing else, the discovery of the ruined church led to a rethink of the supposed founder as St. Cairan of Saighair. Apparently, the altar of the church was elaborately and beautifully decorated with shells and stones which Piran himself had collected all along the Cornish shoreline. A single black stone hearth had formed the centre of his tiny living quarters and it was here that Piran lived and cooked in the fashion of an ancient Celtic holy man. According to legend Piran was sitting behind his hearthstone one night when in the ashes and soot of the fire, he saw a small trickle of silver. This was a trail of tin, and the saint is credited with discovering the element in Cornwall, even though Cornish people had been trading in the metal for centuries before and Roman and Phoenician merchants had bought it there long before Piran arrived. Thus Piran became the patron saint of tinsmiths and the first man in Cornwall to work in the metal.

Virtually nothing is known of Piran's ministry, nor did he leave behind any corpus of religious writings or sayings.

Neither were any substantive *Lives* written concerning him, as with other saints, and much of what we can guess about him dates from the Middle Ages when his cult was at its most powerful and pilgrimages were made to his shrine in Cornwall. Legend says that he died, aged 206 or 216 (obviously an exaggeration) and that he was buried with his mother near to the chapel which he had maintained. It is here that a certain element of paganism appears to creep into the tale. It is said that Piran's head was kept in a reliquary and was displayed for worship at certain times of the year. It is also stated that three human skulls were found close to a nearby well and that three skeletons were found close by. This may have its origins in pagan belief.

Amongst many ancient peoples, the head was considered to be the seat of the soul and so worthy of veneration. Consequently the heads of various great men – wizards and warriors – were frequently displayed and were worshipped in pagan times. These were displayed at wells and stone shrines in the countryside and such practices were frequently condemned by the embryonic Christian church, as they were too strongly associated with paganism. However, the veneration of Piran seems to have contained some elements of this and the cult of the saint may have formed a kind of 'bridge' between the new Christian religion and older traditions. The presence of three skulls and the three decapitated bodies certainly hints at the possibility of some sort of pagan ritual being performed on the nominally Christian site.

Although essentially Cornish, traces of his cult are also to be found in South Wales and in Brittany. The monastic scribe, Gerald of Wales, speaks of a church in Cardiff, which was dedicated to St. Piran. It was here that the English king, Henry II came to celebrate Mass and to give thanks for his victories in Ireland. As he left the church, the king was stopped by a mysterious stranger, dressed in white and carrying a powerful staff who told him that he

must mend his ways and to prohibit trading on Sundays
(then, as now, a holy day of rest) or great misfortune would
befall him. Greatly angered by this impertinence, the king
had his soldiers search for the stranger but to no avail.
Henry chose to disregard the warning and within a year,
he had become embroiled in the murder of Thomas a
Beckett and he died in 1189 knowing that three of his sons,
Richard, Henry and John were all against him. The stranger
who had accosted him was identified with St. Piran himself. This is undoubtedly a medieval fiction, used as a won-
der-tale and to embellish certain events in the Plantagenet
dynasty but it still serves to illustrate the strength of Piran's
cult in the 12th century. Even though there is no record of
the saint ever having even visited Brittany, a flat stone between St. Pol-de-Leon and Lesneven, is still known at 'St.
Piran's Bed' where the saint is supposed to have rested. A
number of hollows in it are said to have been made by his
knees as he prayer fervently for the sins of the world.

It is not known whether or not the saint ever left Cornwall
to visit these place or simply whether his veneration there
was simply due to the spread of his cult in the Middle Ages.
There are stories of him visiting Rome and Jerusalem but
these have no historical accuracy – Celtic saints always
seemed to be visiting these locations, though that is not to
say that some of them did not travel great distances. It is
highly probable, however, that Piran did not leave Cornwall
once he had settled there or if he did, he didn't travel all
that far from it. Followers in later years may have spread
his name to many other locations and dedicated churches
in his name.

On his travels was reputedly accompanied by his first
disciples – not human but a boar, a fox, a badger, a calf and
a doe. As he walked, he was fed by ravens from the air.
This, of course, gives him an affinity with many other Celtic
saints, many of whom were almost the embodiment of the
natural world so close were they to plants and animals.

The legends tell that he was able to cause things to grow or wither through supernatural power. For instance, one story tells of how he passed an applet tree in the depths of winter and, feeling hungry, raised his staff, whereupon the tree gave forth a crop of apples upon which the saint dined. On another occasion, a thorn bush pricked him sorely as he passed by it. Enraged by the wound, the saint turned around and hurled a virulent curse at the growth. It immediately shriveled away under the power of his wrath and never grew again. There are many other such tales of the saint, either bestowing favours or imprecations on both plants and animals for Piran often appears to have been something of a moody and capricious saint.

Unlike some other Celtic saints, there is nothing tangible to really remind us of St. Piran. His bachall (pastoral staff), which was said to have been one of the most ornate in all of Cornwall, covered in gold and studded with precious gems together with a silver pectoral cross which was said to contain tiny relics of the saint have been lost to history. So too has a small processional bell, supposedly made of beaten copper, together with a robe and a tunic. Tradition states that all these treasures were once all held in Cornwall but as locations vary, no one is quite sure where. It is even unclear as to what became of St. Piran's head and its ornate reliquary. It is possible that it may have been destroyed during the Reformation or even during the late medieval period.

At the height of the Middle Ages, 'St Piran's Feast' was kept as a holiday all over Cornwall with much frivolity and celebration. The saint's name also appears in three Cornish parishes – Perran-ar-Worthal, Perranzabuloe and Perranuthnoe. Although a relatively obscure holy man, the name of St. Piran continues to live on.

Chapter 17

WINEFRIDE

Like many other female Celtic saints, St. Winefride is closely associated with healing. The waters of St. Winefride's Well at Treffynnon or Holywell in North Wales have long been said to cure many ailments. Kings, bishops and common people alike have sought their cures and the Well is the only holy shrine in the British Isles to have escaped destruction during the Reformation. In 1629 it was claimed that over 14,000 laity together with members of the clergy had visited the site on pilgrimage in one day (on the saint's Feast Day, 3rd November). Although the number is almost certainly exaggerated, it serves to illustrate the importance of Holywell as a recusant centre. During one period Jesuits were in almost permanent residence there, giving the site added status whilst in 1774, Dr. Johnson saw large numbers of people bathing there. Although the original source of the Well was diverted due to mining operations in the area in 1917, pilgrimages still continue. The well remains open from dawn till dusk and in accordance with tradition, afflicted people pass through the waters three times – perhaps an echo of the ancient Celtic Christian custom of baptism using triple immersion.

St Winefred or Gwenfrewi herself seems to date from around the 7th century and was almost certainly a Welsh princess. She was reputedly the daughter of a prince, Tefydd of Treffynnon (Flintshire) and his wife Gwenlo. She was said to have been a niece of St. Beuno of Gwynned and her cult is believed to have been a subsidiary of his. The *Legend of Winefride* was written by Robert of Shrewsbury when her relics were translated in 1138 but was closely associated with the *Life* of Beuno written in the 14th century. Subsequent versions of it appear all through the 13th, 14th and 15th centuries and it was certainly well known in England as late as the 18th and early 19th centuries when pilgrimage was still fairly well at its height.

In the *Legend*, Winefride is described as a Welsh virgin of considerable beauty who was lustily pursued by a ruthless prince named Caradog from nearby Hawarden. She resisted his advances, declaring that she wished to follow the Christian life. This only served to enrage Caradog who pursued her even more vigorously. Seeing that her protestations were having no effect, Winefride fled. She ran to the door of the Christian church in Treffynnon intending to claim sanctuary there. The door, however, was locked and before it could be opened Caradog had caught up with her. Inflamed with anger and passion, he raised his sword. Just as the church door opened he struck Winefride, cutting her head off. As the body fell away outside the door, the head bounced once and settled inside the building. Immediately, a spring rose on the spot where it had bounced and this is believed to have been the source of the holy well. In horror at what he had done, Caradog fled but the severed head and the body were preserved in the church until the arrival of her uncle St. Beuno who was then a preacher in Clynnog Fawr. The holy man placed the head next to the body and prayed that she be restored to life. His prayers were answered and Winefride was made whole and rose, her life returned and with only a white scar around her neck where Caradog's sword had severed it. Shortly after, Caradog himself was killed in a supernaturally induced earthquake, during which the ground opened up and swallowed him.

One account concerning her subsequent life says that

she returned briefly with Beuno to Clynnog and from there she went to Bodfari, then to Henllan and finally to Gwytherin near Llanrwst, where under instruction from St. Eleri, she founded a missionary station in the remote Welsh mountains. Other sources state that she became abbess of a convent in Treffynnon whilst others still say that she was abbess of the convent at Gwytherin. As a recompense for restoring her to life, St. Beuno requested her to send him a woolen cloak each year on the Feast Day of St. John the Baptist. This was the day upon which she was supposedly brought back to life. The gift was to be placed on a large rock in the middle of a swift flowing river from whence it would be carried by angels directly to Beuno. Winefride was to pray for this miracle and it would happen. Other sources tell how the stone moved down the river, bearing the dry cloak to her uncle.

There is no date given as to when Winefride eventually died except for the hint that she was very old when she did. The date of her death is often given as 22nd June but the year is unknown, although it is sometimes given as AD 680 (although there is a tradition that a small *Life* – long since lost – was written about her in 660, 'a long time after she was dead'). Her relics were retained in Treffynnon until 1138 when they were removed to the Benedictine abbey at Shrewsbury for safekeeping. It was there that the prior Robert added details of her story to the *Life of Bueno* that he was writing.

In the early Middle Ages, the cult of Winefride was mainly confined to the North Welsh Marches and to the districts of Euias and Erging in the south. It was certainly flourishing there in the mid-12th century but all the evidence points to the survival of a far older cult in several parts of Wales. It was not until 1398 that she enjoyed a wider popularity in England. This was due to Roger Walden who was Archbishop of Canterbury during the exile of Thomas Arundel. He had heard the miraculous story of

Winefride and was greatly impressed. Her link with St. Beuno did not disadvantage her either. In 1415, Walden's successor, Henry Chichele, a former bishop of St. David's and a man with a great interest in Welsh saints, raised the name of St. Winefride to a higher rank with a Feast Day on 3rd November. About the same time both Holywell and Shrewsbury were increasing in importance as pilgrim destinations and Winefride benefited from the increased local interest. She also benefited from small changes in the liturgy which some of these pilgrims brought with them and from the establishment of well-defined and important pilgrim roads through both Holywell and Shrewsbury. There were several shrines round about and pilgrims could now visit them all on a single visit whilst making Holywell a centre for their journey. This was of course, good for the area and to encourage this, a pilgrim guesthouse was built at Ludlow.

As the legend of Winefride grew in the 14th and 15th centuries together with the curative properties of her holy well, the number of pilgrims to 'take the waters' increased and the site became a major stopping place on many pilgrimages. The well received a Royal seal of approval during the 15th century when King Henry V made a pilgrimage on foot from Shrewsbury to use the waters in 1416; whilst although there is no record of it, Edward IV is supposed to have done the same. It is also said that Lady Margaret Beaufort, mother of Henry VII took the waters there during pregnancy. She certainly knew of Holywell and seems to have been taken by it as she built a fine chapel there, which is still extant. This was built directly after the Battle of Bosworth Field in 1485. It may have been this connection to Lady Margaret which saved the site during the worst of the Reformation when he grandson, Henry VIII sought to destroy such places. Certainly pilgrimages continued and cures were affected during the height of the period and continued well into the 18th and 19th centuries.

St Winefride's Well was certainly considered to be one of the premier healing sites in England and Wales from the medieval period onwards. Soon only the shrine of Our Lady of Walsingham was a more important site on the pilgrim trail than Holywell.

By the 1890s', the healing properties of the well waters were so firmly established in the public mind that a thriving religious export industry had grown up around it. Bottled water taken from the spring was being sent all over the Celtic world. An advert in the *Holywell Record* (a small magazine produced for pilgrims) in 1st May 1890 cites:

> 'St Winefride's Well, Holywell. A bottle of water can be sent post free to any part of the United Kingdom Send Postal Order for One Shilling to Father Beauclerk S.J., Holywell N. Wales. And give your address clearly'.

A testimonial in the same magazine, praises the miraculous powers of the water:

> 'A client of St. Winefride writes from Charlestown, Co. Mayo, Ireland:
> "Reverend Sir – Kindly send me per return more water. The previous water has wrought wonderful cures here'."

Theses bottles were, apparently, actually moulded in a styles form of St. Winefride. Father Beauclerk, a resident Jesuit priest, had done much to promote the notion of the cures from the Well and had almost single handedly restored the numbers of visiting pilgrims to medieval levels.

Like, perhaps, the possibly contemporaneous story of St. Dympna, the Legend of Winefride may be no more than a medieval romance, which was popular during the middle Ages. Certainly it contains many of the classical motifs which are current in such tales – the chaste virgin, the lecherous and brutal suitor and the miraculous event that restores her to life and health. Perhaps that is what appealed to the pilgrims who visited her shrine. And once again, pagan elements feature in the story. As in the history of St. Pirin, heads feature in the story. Some versions of the story recount that when St. Beuno lifted Winefride's severed head, it spoke to him and actually told him secrets of the Life to Come, of the forces that govern the world and how Death could be conquered through special prayers. These were the prayers that the holy man used in order to restore her to life and which have influenced the healing waters of her Well. The worship of heads, especially at wells or in watery places, was important to the ancient Celts and this belief may well have left its mark on the Christianised story of Winefride. There are even some suggestions that, prior to her restoration by St. Beuno, a female head may have been worshipped at a Well in Treffynnog prior to the coming of Christianity.

Certainly the story of the stoical Winefride and the renown of her supernatural curing spring has inspired many down the centuries. It may have appealed to the sense of the mystical which lies deep within every one of us and which is the foundation of religion. As has already been mentioned, the noted Doctor Johnson was greatly amazed at the numbers that flocked to avail of the curative properties of the waters and the well-known poet Gerard Manley Hopkins (1844–89) also took an interest in the site. Intrigued by the legend of St. Winefride he penned a poetic play, which was published in a collection of his poems in 1918 and entitled *St. Winefred's Well*. In it, and through the mouth of St. Beuno, he details some of the ailments that the waters of the Well were said to cure:

'Stone, palsy, cancer, cough lung wasting, womb not
bearing,
Rupture, running sores, what more?'

And he brings his poem-play almost to a close by celebrating the widespread renown of the Well:

'Here to this holy well shall pilgrimages be,
And not from purple Wales only nor from elmy England,
But from beyond seas, Erin, France and Flanders, everywhere
Pilgrims, still pilgrims, more pilgrims, still more poor pilgrims
What sights shall be when some that swung, wretches on
   crutches
Their crutches shall cast from them, on heels of air de-
   parting',

St. Winefride is usually depicted in art with a bubbling spring at her feet. She still remains a romantic and mysterious figure amongst the catalogue of Celtic saints.

Chapter 18

WINWALOE

Although often counted as temperamental and extremely austere, the sixth-century Breton Saint Winwaloe or Guenole, was instrumental in forging links between Cornwall and Brittany and thus strengthening the ties which bound both the British and Continental Celtic worlds together. His name meaning 'he who is fair' appears a little ironic when considering this sometimes irascible, extremely austere and rather inflexible holy man.

Winwaloe was born into a Celtic Cornish family, which seems to have fled to Brittany, leaving behind coastal estates that were under attack by the Saxons. He was born near St. Brieuc, the third son of the family. Allegedly his parents, both Christians, had promised that if they were granted a third son, he would be dedicated to the service of God. However, it was said that Winwaloe – who was strong-willed and obstinate even then – baulked at the idea of entering a monastery and it was not until he was fifteen years of age that he and his two brothers, Gwethenoc and Jacut, set out to join the foundation of St. Budoc on the island of 'Laruea' (probably Lavret, a region of the Ile de Brehat.

The monastic life proved too much for his two brothers who shortly returned home but Winwaloe took to Holy Orders and stayed on. He studied under the tutelage of Budoc, a venerable and well-respected teacher, and he proved himself to be an extremely capable student. At the end of his studies, Winwaloe was sent out as part of a party of twelve, to seek out and found a new monastery or mission station, which would spread the Gospel in pagan areas.

Tradition states that they landed on the island of Tibidy where they planned to found their holy house. For three years they enduring hardship – the ground was salty and infertile and only scant crops could grow there; the island was buffeted by fierce winds and parts of it were subject to high tides which washed some of the monks plantings away – but eventually the majority of the Brothers decided to abandon the site. Winwaloe however stayed on, living the austere life of a simple hermit. He lived on roots and herbs that grew on the interior of the island and he tried to grow some barley crop. The severity of the winds made such an enterprise impossible and eventually even he had to think of an alternative site.

It is said that one evening when on the island's shore, he beheld angels ascending and descending to and from the opposite shore of the River Aulne where in a vision, he saw trees laden with fruit and beautiful waterfalls. He decided to go there, setting ashore at a placed named Landevennec, which became the name of his monastery.

An alternative version of the above legend states that the island of Tibidy was actually an earthly Paradise that had been touched by God. Because of this, no one could die there and the monks enjoyed eternal life which some of them could not bear. So they returned to the mainland in order that they might be granted a release from immortality. Most of them joined Winwaloe when he set up his monastery on the shores of the Aulne. The land for the foundation was granted by Geadlon, who had estates at Tevenec along the River. Gradlon's tomb can still be seen at Landevennec.

There are a number of peculiar legends linking Winwaloe with the lost kingdom of Lyonaise (Lyonesse). This was a fabulous kingdom which was said to stretch from the French coast and into Cornwall and which was overwhelmed by the sea, now forming part of the English Channel. The country was supposed to be extremely pleasant and was ruled over by a number of kings of whom Gradlon is sometimes counted as one (although this is improbable). Winwaloe (in his incarnation of Guenole) is sometimes cited ax the patron saint of Lyonaise and it was said that he was consulted by its various kings on matters concerning religion. He is also said to have established several monastic foundations in that country – the largest close to the foot of St. Michael's Mount (supposedly the tallest peak in Lyonaise), which is now under the sea. These are probably all fanciful stories but they serve to demonstrate the closeness of the south of England and Brittany in both religious and secular terms.

As in a number of other Celtic monasteries, the regime at Landevennec was extremely rigid and severe. Wine was forbidden except at the Mass, with only water being served to drink. There was barley bread to eat, together with raw or boiled roots, except on the Sabbath and certain feast days when cheese and shellfish could be eaten. Winwaloe himself wore a tunic of rough goatskin and he insisted that his followers do the same. Like St. David, he insisted on standing for long periods in a freezing river (in Winwaloe's case, the River Aulne) reciting the Psalter and with his arms completely outstretched to emulate the Cross. Several of his monks did likewise but when others complained, Winwaloe insisted that they be whipped for their disobedience to God's Will. He was not a man to be argued with; and in Landevennec his word was law.

For their beds, the Brothers used the barks of trees with a stone for a pillow and each of them was required to work on the land for several hours every day. This harsh Rule – known as the Rule of Winwaloe – was kept at Landevennec until the year 818, when Louis the Pious, the son of the

Emperor Charlemagne, revoked it and supplanted it with the Rule of St. Benedict. Landevennec remains a Benedictine abbey today.

Part of the diet at Winwaloe's foundation consisted of fish, which had doubtless been caught in the river beside the monastery. It was said that God granted Winwaloe a bell which if rang would draw fish from all over to be caught in the monks' net and in this way Winwaloe (who had now been appointed abbot) was able to feed the monastery. The sound of this bell was said never to fail and that fishes followed it in shoals, but to the regret of fishermen everywhere, it has since been lost – if it ever existed in the first place.

Although Winwaloe is often celebrated for his charity and patience, other accounts describe him as a temperamental and abrasive character. Those who disagreed with him were either subject to a stream of abuse or a long and sonorous sermon on their own failings. He would not sit down in church preferring to walk about, prostrate himself or simply stand. His character seems to have been a restless and turbulent one. He could, legend says, be extremely moody for a holy man and many of the young novices were actually afraid of him because he could be subject to temper tantrums. As with many of us, as he grew older, his temper seemed to grow much shorter.

There are many disputes as to when St. Winwaloe actually died and at what age. Some accounts of his life give his age at over 200 years old, others place him at more than 300, but it is known that he died on the 3rd March, which became his Feast Day. He was buried at Landevennec where he had been abbot. The earliest *Life* of St. Winwaloe was written around the 9th century. This was *La Legende Doree de Saint-Guenole*, which was reputedly set down by a monk Clement who had been a novice at Landevennec and which details a number of miracles and sayings attributed to the saint.

In AD 914, Vikings attacked and completely destroyed

Landevennec and most of the relics of St. Winwaloe – his body, vestments and a hand bell (sadly not the one with which he summoned the fishes) – were temporarily removed, first to Chateau-du-Loir and from there to Montreuil-sur-Mer near Boulogne. Later they were returned and enshrined in a new church on the 28th April 960, although the date in unclear and some calendars give 26th February as the time of the saint's translation. Certain other of Winwaloe's unspecified relics were taken to Mont-Blandin near Ghent in Belgium and were never returned.

Despite being a Breton saint, Winwaloe had a vigorous following and a widespread cult in England. The reason for this was twofold – several monastic foundations in Cornwall from his abbey in Landvennec and the spread of his relics. Two Cornish churches still bear his name – Landewednack and the 'Church of the Storms' at Gunwalloe, which derives its name from the fact that it is built virtually on a beach at the mercy of wind and sea. Both of these sites are on the Lizard. His name also occurs in English litanies of the 10th and 11th centuries when his cult must have been at its height. Exeter, Glastonbury, Abington and Waltham all claimed to have some of his relics in their possession at one time or another and his name frequently occurs in a number of English church calendars from the late 12th century.

St. Dunstan's exile to Mont-Blandin on the accession of the Saxon King Edwy of Wessex in the year 955 and his subsequent return to England two years later, probably also encouraged the spread of Winwaloe's cult across England, together with relic gifts to Leofric, Bishop of Exeter. It is said that Dunstan may have presented a jeweled crozier, known as St. Winwaloe's Staff to the West-Saxon King Edger around the year 958, which had been previously housed at a monastery in Brittany.

Like the Bachall of St. Patrick (the Beculum Jesu) it had been given to Winwaloe by an angel and was said to have great supernatural powers. What became of this relic is unknown. Winwaloe's feast was celebrated in East Anglia and in Norwich, where a street was named after him commemorating the dedication of a church there.

His temperamental and often volatile nature is also recorded in an old piece of weather doggerel. The saint's Feast Day, 3rd March, fell directly after the Feast Days of two other saints, David of Wales and Chad of Lichfield (1st and 2nd March respectively). Hence the rhyme ran:

'First comes David, then comes Chad,
Then comes Winnol, roaring mad'

The implication was, of course, that the saint's unpredictable and stormy temperament had transferred itself to the weather of the third day of March. The couplet was widely used as a folk weather gauge right across England all through the Middle Ages and even into the 18th and possibly early 19th centuries. Old people would shun 'St. Winnol's Day', 3rd March, for the commencement of any important task, as its outcome was sure to be uncertain or unprofitable.

St. Winwaloe is portrayed on an altar-screen at Portlemouth in Devon with his bell with which he called the fish but it is in Cornwall where he seems to have had most influence. Although there is really no evidence for the belief, it is said that he returned there for a time and that he had a hermitage for a time somewhere on the Lizard (the site of which is often given as Castle Hill near Gunwalloe) where he carried out many miracles, mainly healing those sick people who came to visit him.

He is also claimed as the patron saint of Towedneck in West Penwith. In medieval times, the site was one of pilgrimage, drawing people from many parts of England and Brittany and a 'pattern day' (a day dedicated to a patron saint) was held. It is not absolutely clear if this day was held on the saint's actual Feast Day or the day of the translation of his remains (or possibly a combination of both). In 1987 this tradition was revived in the town in which the abbot and monks presently worshipping at Landevennec were invited to attend.

Thus, the links, which Winwaloe had forged back in the 6th century, had been celebrated in the present day – a fitting tribute to a remarkable saint.

BIBLIOGRAPHY

A Little Book of Celtic Saints Martin Wallace, Appletree Press, 1995

Carmina Gadelica Alexander Carmichael, Floris, 1992

Celtic Saints Dara Delap (Ann Lockhart, ed), Pitkin Pictorial, 1995

Columbanus in His Own Words Cardinal Tomas O'Fiaich, Veritas, 1974

Early Christian Ireland Liam and Moira de Paor, Thames & Hudson, 1991

Irish Shrines and Reliquaries of the Middle Ages Raghnall O'Floinn, County House in Association with the National Museum of Ireland, 1994

Malachy A. Brian Scott, Veritas, 1976

The Day to Day Life of the Desert Fathers in Fourth Century Egypt Lucien Regnault, St. Bede's Publications, 1999

Wisdom of the Celtic Saints Edward S. Selner, Ave Maria Press, 1993